To

Doug and Charleene

*"We've a Story to tell
to the Nations"*

See How Jesus
Handled Rejection!

People Even Jesus Failed to Reach

With Interactive Study Guide

John 10:10, 11

Gerald H. Ihle

See How Jesus Handled Rejection!

People Even Jesus Failed to Reach
With Interactive Study Guide

Gerald H. Ihle

WINEPRESS **WP** PUBLISHING

Packaged by WinePress Publishing, PO Box 428, Enumclaw, WA 98022. The views expressed or implied in this work do not necessarily reflect those of WinePress Publishing. The author is ultimately responsible for the design, content, and editorial accuracy of this work.

Unless otherwise noted all scriptures are taken from the Revised Standard Version of the Bible. © 1946, 1952, 1971 by the Division of Christian Education of the National Council of the Churches of Christ in the U.S.A. Used by permission.

ISBN 1-57921-719-2
Library of Congress Catalog Card Number: 2003111888

"After this many of His disciples drew back and no longer went about with Him."

John 6:66

"He was despised and rejected by men . . ."

Isaiah 53:3

Cover Picture

The cover picture is from a painting by the Italian Artist, Antonio Ciseri, entitled "Ecce Homo" or "Behold the Man." The picture portrays Jesus before Pilate, the Roman governor who condemned Jesus to crucifixion. Ciseri died in Florence, Italy in 1891.

ACKNOWLEDGMENTS

With sincere thanks to my dear wife, Janet, who offered countless suggestions, corrections, and criticisms of this manuscript. You sat with me for hours debating, line by line, the ideas expressed in this book and helped me to get them down. Your patience and love have been boundless . . .

Many thanks also to Mrs. Joetta Learn, who typed the original manuscript; to Mrs. Nancy J. Kessler, who transcribed it onto computer disk; to Tammy Hopf, my Project Manager at WinePress Publishing; to my editor, Simeon Spillane—Without your able assistance, this book may never have been completed.

Finally, I want to thank Bishop Neil L. Irons, United Methodist Resident Bishop of the Harrisburg Area of Pennsylvania, for taking the time to read my manuscript and to write the Foreword to my book.

CONTENTS

FOREWORD

Evangelism, the work of sharing the gospel beyond the circle of believers, is the work of the church. Too often believers seem under the impression that if they can just say the right words or use the correct formula, that every response will be positive. Gerald Ihle's book sets the record straight on that score. Looking carefully at Jesus through the eyes of the Gospels, the author points to the fact that even our Lord did not achieve universal acceptance from His hearers.

This book frees the disciple from worrying about "success" and shifts the emphasis on evangelism to bearing witness to the Good News. Fortunately, the believer is put back in the correct place of being called to share with others, rather than being anxious about her/his results. This may seem a subtle shift to the casual reader, but it is a necessary correction to the place of bearing testimony to God's care for those outside the church.

After all, it is finally the Holy Spirit which translates the words and deeds of the followers of Jesus to the hearer. The Christian is privileged to share the news of God's mercy and love without having a false expectation that everyone is ready to respond affirmatively to them. The mission is to bear witness, not to calculate an achievement percentage. Instead of focusing on rejection, the following pages are actually an encouragement to those who would speak a word for God and perform some healing ministry to another.

Here is a kind of realism that remains optimistic in a world of people that does not always welcome gospel. In analyzing the reasons that some responded negatively to Jesus, Ihle directs the reader to those joyful moments when, in spite of stiff resistance around Him, Jesus brings about dramatic life conversions and healings. His purpose in these pages is to assure the would-be bearer of the gospel that rejection never has the last word. God does. Thank heaven!

—Bishop Neil L. Irons, Ph.D.
The United Methodist Church,
Harrisburg Area, Pennsylvania
Resident Bishop
Former Bishop New Jersey Area

PREFACE

This is a book on Christian evangelism with a different slant than usual. It is not a new "how-to" book by a church growth expert with all the answers or tips on how to be more persuasive in winning people to Jesus Christ. Rather, it is meant to be a reminder that sometimes no matter how well something is communicated or presented, some people will remain unchanged by its message.

Some are turned off by organized religion of any kind. Some just don't *want* to be serious followers of Jesus Christ or to be part of His Church in this world. In His lifetime, some walked away from Jesus; others resisted Him and rejected His claims or His hard demands. Others hated Him so much that they religiously justified even the act of killing Him.

This book reminds readers that in spite of Jesus' gifted ability to attract great crowds with the miracles He performed and the amazing teachings He conveyed, even Jesus Christ was unable to reach many of the people He was trying to persuade. Is it any wonder that modern believers experience the same kinds of rejection as our Lord?

The Gospel account reminds us that Jesus sometimes offended people so much with His claims and teachings that even his own disciples walked away and left Him. Once Jesus used the metaphor of bread in an effort to explain His mission, but His reference to Himself as the "Bread of Life" offended many listeners.

"After this many of His disciples drew back and no longer went with Him" (John 6:66).

What church wouldn't be upset to see members leaving because of disagreements with the pastoral leadership? In the Gospel account, the Lord of the Church was offending people and losing disciples because of what He was saying. This couldn't be an effective "church growth" technique! It seemed more like an unsuccessful strategy resulting in decline, like a failure to keep one's followers satisfied—hardly an inspired leadership plan!

Is there anything to be learned from this apparent "failure?"

My intent in writing this book is to encourage clergy and laity alike, who often get terribly discouraged with the inability to fill church pews on Sunday mornings. So many churches and Sunday Schools in America have experienced decline for one reason or another, while still others experience growth, spiritual vitality, and a sense of mission. *Why?*

It is easy for Christians to identify numerically growing, successful churches as authentic discipleship groups, while churches that are declining in membership seem marked by a failure in discipleship and a failure in vision. Such an attitude overlooks something very important, however.

Sometimes Jesus Christ modeled growth and success. But at other times, Jesus failed to get people to follow Him. The Bible record is clear: He was not always successful in reaching people. *Many* rejected Jesus as Messiah and Savior. Biblical stories also remind us that the blame for this failure of response lay not with Christ, but with the hearer.

Think about it. Many behaviors can be taught or required, but you can't force *love* or *faith*. Jesus experienced the same frustration with people that modern Christians have with those who reject the invitation to welcome Christ and His call to Christian discipleship.

Christians should not really be surprised to have the *same* experience that Jesus had at times in reaching people, young and old. Yet rather than giving up, we need to follow Jesus' example, accept rejection, and turn to others who are *ready* to respond eagerly to the call to become believers and followers of Christ.

Strangely, many Christians would have a hard time admitting that Jesus Christ ever *failed* at anything. After all, He *did* attract crowds by the thousands and performed amazing miracles of healing for people of all ages. *How could the triumphant Messiah ever fail at anything?*

Obviously, Christ's followers would often fail to be as successful as the Master. The Gospel account documents the fact of that reality, even for the apostles. When comparing the results of their efforts with those of the Master or with those of seemingly more successful Christian leaders or churches, Christians can often feel like failures. But let's examine that self-evaluation and seek Christ's definition of success and failure.

More than anything else, this is a book for *struggling* Christians who are not reaping outward success at every turn, who look out over too many empty pews on Sunday morning and see empty Sunday school rooms that should be bulging with children and teenagers, seniors and adults.

It is so easy to conclude that the reason many choose to abandon the Christian way is due to faulty Christians and imperfect churches. Clergy and laity alike can thus feel guilty over the ineffectiveness of today's church in reaching our modern technological and secular society—to say nothing of people who follow other world religions.

Many churches just don't seem to grow, even though surrounded by fast-growing communities mushrooming all around them. In a success-oriented society, it is discouraging not to be able to succeed in reaching more people for Jesus Christ.

Many fine, committed Christian parents find that their own children have lost interest in church and in religious values. Some teenagers have turned their backs on religious instruction. Often it seems American families are too busy for church. Bible study is totally disregarded by ever- so-many, thus biblical illiteracy is rampant in our land.

Meanwhile, society is paying a big price for the church's inability to bring the nation to its knees before God, as it had been able to do at times in past history. Indeed, too many have lost the very fear of God.

No matter what new strategies, changes in worship services, innovations in communication systems, attractive programs, or changing leadership churches offer, there still remains the frustrating realization that Christians are not reaching *the crowd* that is still *out there*, "like sheep without a shepherd" (Mark 6:34). As a pastor for forty-three years, I have often asked myself the questions, "What is wrong with the church? What more should we be doing? What is wrong with *me?*"

As the ancient prophets had failed in their day to reach people with God's message, so Jesus Himself sensed His inability to turn Jerusalem from its stubborn resistance to God's ways. He lamented, "O Jerusalem, Jerusalem, killing the prophets and stoning those who are sent to you! How often would I have gathered your children together as a hen gathers her brood under her wings, and you would not!" (Matthew 23:37)

How Jesus handled rejection is the subject of our focus here. Since Jesus often experienced rejection by the people He was trying to reach, the same as Christians today, perhaps there is a *lesson* that can be learned from the Master on how we can handle the rejection that we experience.

Who hasn't experienced rejection of some sort in life—whether in dating, within marriage and family, or after a job interview? Authors, musicians, actors, admissions applicants to colleges, scholarship contenders, and applicants for loans or new home mortgages often experience rejection.

Even children and teenagers have experienced rejection by their peers for many reasons. We must learn to handle rejection as a common experience of living—one that can mold our character and honor God when properly endured.

Rejection can be terribly damaging and discouraging to the ego, making one feel like a failure in life instead of a success. Yet, in spite of multiple rejections and even threats on His life, Jesus kept on course with His mission to redeem a lost world that was not always receptive to His invitations, claims, and warnings.

Even so, we must not let our inability to touch *all* of the lives around us discourage us so much that we stop reaching out to those who *will* receive our efforts with gratitude, with joy, and with saving faith.

Chapter One

THE REJECTED CORNERSTONE

"The stone that the builders rejected has become the head of the corner."

—Psalm 118:22

It is hard to picture the Lord Jesus Christ, the "Miracle Worker," failing at anything. It is much easier to admit our own failures as His followers. We need to be reminded that Jesus had the same problem we do in reaching people who are indifferent, doubtful, ignorant, or even hostile to the Christian Gospel. Some not only turned their backs on Jesus, but also wanted to destroy Him and His teachings and claims. Jesus met some of His worst opposition from religious people!

Christ was always up-front with His followers, reminding them often that they would experience success as well as failure, acceptance as well as rejection, as they tried to win over the world for His Kingdom. The Lord Jesus told His followers plainly, "Remember the word that I said to you, 'A servant is not greater than his master.' If they persecuted me, they will persecute you; if they kept my word, they will keep yours also" (John 15:20).

There were always people Jesus could not persuade or convince, no matter how hard He tried. It should come as no surprise to us when we, His followers, meet similar resistance. As He ministered to the generation of His time, one thing became very clear: success would not necessarily be the badge of authenticity. In fact, according to Jesus, popular acclaim and success might only point to a compromising prophet, a *false* prophet.

"Woe to you, when all men speak well of you, for so their fathers did to the false prophets" (Luke 6:26).

False prophets can look very successful as they attract many followers. Jesus, on the other hand, was preparing *His* followers to see that all people would not speak well of Him, that many would reject Him, how ever unbelievable that might seem.

To illustrate this truth, Jesus told one of His many stories, a common parable. The story was about a vineyard leased out to tenants after the vines had been planted. Its owner expected payments from the tenants and sent his servants to collect from them. But the tenants refused to make the payments and beat the collectors, ignoring their lease agreement.

This happened several times. In desperation, the vineyard owner sent his son to receive payment. Surely, he reasoned, they would have respect for the son of the owner and pay up. But the tenants killed the son. Now there would be no heir to the vineyard. The grieving father was in a rage and became determined to have his revenge.

"He will come and destroy those tenants, and give the vineyard to others," Jesus' story continues (Luke 20:16).

Interestingly, just after Jesus told this story, He made reference to a cornerstone that some builders had rejected.

By the use of this metaphor, He was implying that He Himself was that cornerstone, as well as the son in the vineyard story.

"The very stone which the builders rejected has become the head of the corner" (Luke 20:17).

Like the son in the story, Jesus would also die. But like the cornerstone, rejection could never destroy Him forever. The cornerstone would outlast rejection. The religious leaders of His day were intent on building their religion *without* the cornerstone, without Jesus as their Messianic King, without Jesus as Savior and Lord. They understood too well that Jesus' entire story was directed against them. They were so enraged, the Bible says, that they would have attacked Him on the spot had it not been for the fact that they feared His supporters.

From this time on, the Scribes and Pharisees would try to entrap Jesus in something He might say in order that they might be justified in having Him destroyed. This would be the beginning of the conspiracy to have Jesus crucified.

> The scribes and the chief priests tried to lay hands on Him at that very hour, but they feared the people; for they perceived that He had told this parable against them. (Luke 20:19)

Jesus made grim predictions that He would have to experience rejection. The vision of success is what usually draws people, but here Jesus talked openly about failure. *Why is this?*

When He was talking about Himself as the cornerstone, which architecturally becomes the chief stone of a building, He was not talking *failure*; He was talking ultimate success and victory.

See How Jesus Handled Rejection!

Jesus gave Simon a new name, Peter, which means *rock*. Yet that rock crumbled under accusations when, three times, Peter fearfully denied that he was one of Jesus' followers. It is interesting to note that Peter, the rock, after his restoration by the resurrected Christ, referred to Jesus as "that living stone rejected by men" (1 Peter 2:4). Peter went on to say that Christ's followers should *all* become "living stones" (1 Peter 2:5).

After the day of Pentecost Peter referred to Jesus Christ as the *rejected stone.*

"This is the stone which was rejected by you builders, but which has become the head of the corner. And there is salvation in no one else" (Acts of the Apostles 4:11–12).

Some of the great hymns of the Christian Church portray Jesus as the Rock. Examples would be, "Rock of Ages" by Augustus M. Toplady; "Christ, the Solid Rock" by Edward Mote, and that great lyric, "Beneath the cross of Jesus I fain would take my stand, the shadow of a mighty rock within a weary land," by Elizabeth C. Clephane.

This Rock is the same Rock, the cornerstone, that Jesus predicted would be scorned by the world. How true that prediction was—as today nation after nation build their societies without the Cornerstone!

Many societies and world religions reject Jesus Christ as the exclusive cornerstone, regarding Jesus as only *one* stone among many, one religious teacher or prophet among others. Governments have been built, economies designed, educational systems devised, laws and cultures created, without the *Cornerstone* in mind. The chaos of history's record demonstrates that something truly is missing. Even today there remains the fearful potential of nuclear, biological, or chemical annihilation of our foundationless world, which recognizes little in the way of moral absolutes.

Jesus was fully perceptive of reality when He predicted that the Cornerstone would be rejected. Even so, the Cornerstone, Jesus Christ, has been welcomed by countless millions of believers over the years who have accepted Him as the Center of their lives and looked forward to a future age when He would be universally recognized as King of Kings, Lord of Lords, and Prince of Peace.

Jesus taught His followers to pray for that time to come, saying to His Father, "Thy kingdom come, Thy will be done." The Apostolic Church lifted up Christ as the cornerstone of the Christian Church. Believers within every generation are responsible to keep that cornerstone in place.

The Church must continually demonstrate that Jesus Christ truly is the Head of the Church while the world protests that the Cornerstone is not necessary and does not fit into its culture. When Jesus predicted His own rejection—and that which His followers would experience—He was merely foretelling an unfortunate reality. The world *did* crucify God's Son. And crowds *still* reject the Christ and His followers. But until Christ returns as the Messianic King, the words of a Biblical prophet remind believers of a rejected man of sorrows, who Christians believe is Jesus.

> He was despised and rejected by men; a man of sorrows and acquainted with grief, and as one whom men hide their faces. He was despised, and we esteemed Him not. (Isaiah 53:3)

Rejection is a fact of life. Even Jesus was not able to reach everyone. Christ's rejection did not only include the scorners who walked away from Him but also those who hated Him enough to kill Him. Knowing this would be so, Jesus *prepared* His followers for resistance and rejection, as well as for success and ultimate victory. Rejection and even hateful hostility should come as no surprise to believers today. We must learn to work through rejection and discouragement, fight the good fight of faith, and savor the successes that do come.

Chapter Two

HIS OWN PEOPLE

"He came to His own home, and His own people received Him not."

—*John 1:11*

As much as we hate to admit it, it seems clear that the Christian Church of our time is failing to reach the masses in America and many parts of the world.

Even though Christianity is the largest world religion, in fact the largest percentage of the world's population is not Christian. Millions of people, including those who profess belief in the world's great religions, such as Judaism, Islam, Hinduism, and Buddhism, do not believe that Jesus is the Son of God, nor the Messianic King, nor the Savior of the world. At best, the great religions will concede that Jesus was a great religious teacher, prophet, apostle, no greater than other religious teachers, and certainly less important than Moses or Muhammad.

The secular world has also turned its back on Jesus. Include in this many acquaintances, relatives, spouses,

family members, and neighbors of professing Christians—
to say nothing of apathetic or hostile former church members who walk no longer in the faith among the community
of believers. That leaves a lot of people out of church. So
many today are too busy for church and turn their backs
on organized religion.

Many disregard the best efforts of faithful Christians
who encourage them to come to church. As a result of
such disinterest, church leaders become discouraged.
Many churches *are* full, thank God! But too many churches
are half (or less) empty on Sunday mornings and too many
have closed.

Some mega-churches have incredible success in reaching the masses, yet many churches just plod on year after
year, unable to make any real inroads into the community.
New housing developments go up all around the country.
But all too often local churches do not reflect the growth in
the community. Their children and teenagers are no longer
found in the nation's Sunday Schools and churches.

Secularism seems to have succeeded in drawing many
parents and their families away from church. Sunday sports,
shopping malls, travel, family outings, work, hobbies, yard
maintenance, and home improvements have displaced old
time religious commitment and eager discipleship.

Obviously there is no preacher or church that is able to
please everyone. "Church shoppers" looking for the perfect church, the perfect preacher, the best choir, make the
rounds—announcing where the "hottest" religious show
can be located. This futile search for the perfect church can
result in cynicism about organized religion.

Certainly, the faithful recognize many of the church's
failings. Pastors and church leaders realize they cannot satisfy everyone with worship styles, choice of music, church
programs, missions outreach, preaching, or congregational

financial decisions. Then there is the problem faithful parents have with restless sons and daughters who have not made a religious commitment. It is discouraging for the faithful to watch the young reject the faith and organized religion. What can be more frustrating than feeling that one has failed to convince those of one's own family?

Jesus knew the frustration of being rejected at home among His own people. He experienced rejection in His home town of Nazareth. The scripture says, "He came to His own home and His own people received Him not" (John 1:11). Christ's rejection by the people of Nazareth went even further.

> And they rose up and put Him out of the city and led Him to the brow of the hill on which the city was built, that they might throw Him down headlong. (Luke 4:29)

Jesus was having a problem winning His own Jewish community and religious home base. It is true that He attracted great crowds of people in some places. But it is also true that in other places countless people turned their backs on Him and walked away. Scripture tells us that, at various times, ". . . many of His disciples drew back and no longer went with him" (John 6:66).

In fact, Jesus failed to win the holy city, Jerusalem, the home of the great Jewish Temple. He agonized over the city's rejection of His efforts:

> O Jerusalem, Jerusalem, killing the prophets and stoning those who are sent to you! How often would I have gathered your children together as a hen gathers her brood under her wings, and you would not! (Matthew 23:37)

What could have been lacking in Christ's efforts? As believers, we would testify that the problem was not Jesus.

It had to be *the people* who rejected Him. Jesus Himself saw the problem as spiritual blindness and ignorance. Again, He laments to those who will not hear Him:

> And when He drew near and saw the city He wept over it, saying, "Would that even today you knew the things that make for peace! But now they are hidden from your eyes." (Luke 19:41–42)

Because they were spiritually blind, they blocked Christ's efforts to reach them with His love. Before Jesus ever sent His disciples out to the Gentiles He sent them first to the people of Israel. "To the Jew first," was always His priority, as the following scripture reveals:

> These twelve Jesus sent out, charging them, "Go no-where among the Gentiles, and enter no town of the Samaritans, but go rather to the lost sheep of Israel." (Matthew 10:5)

We like to think of Jesus as a Christian, but Jesus was a Hebrew; He was Jewish. *We* are Christians. Jesus' parents were Jews. He was raised in the Jewish faith. He attended the synagogue and the Temple, not a church. He showed forth His Jewish heritage when He told a Samaritan woman that, "Salvation is from the Jews." (John 4:22)

Jesus came to His own people, the Jews, and many of them *did* believe that He was the promised Messiah. But as we know others, including the religious leaders of His day, rejected Him. It is disheartening to be rejected by one's own people. When Jesus realized He offended His people He told them, "A prophet is not without honor, except in His own country, and among His own kin, and in His own house" (Mark 6:4). The Scripture says He marveled because of their unbelief.

Familiarity bred only contempt for Jesus in His hometown of Nazareth. It was difficult for the townspeople there to see greatness in this son of a local carpenter. After all, they knew His parents, as well as His brothers and sisters, as their lifelong neighbors and as fellow citizens.

"Is not this the carpenter, the son of Mary and brother of James and Joses and Judas and Simon, and are not His sisters with us?" (Mark 6:3), they asked.

John's Gospel tells us that those of Christ's own household had trouble believing in Him.

"For even His brothers did not believe in Him" (John 7:5).

Jesus' was just too familiar a face to be considered special. He lacked the mystique of an out-of-town celebrity. The neighbors had known Jesus since He was a boy playing in the streets of Nazareth or helping His father, Joseph, in his carpentry shop. How in the world could a small town carpenter be the Messianic King?

The Jewish people lived with the hope of a Messiah who would come to deliver them from all enemies and set up a utopian kingdom. They were looking for a military Messiah, not a hometown boy who was now spending His time doing medical work healing sick people and teaching.

When God sent a Messianic King, would He send a carpenter or a military general, they wondered. And instead of troops to defeat the Romans, this King Jesus had fishermen, right off the boat from Galilee! A Messianic King should be riding triumphantly and proudly into Jerusalem on top of a white horse, not walking dusty roads with unarmed followers.

Jesus finally did ride into Jerusalem, but not on a white horse with an army. He rode in on a lowly donkey—with His followers waving palm leaves, not swords. On the day Jesus went to the Cross and afterward, the Roman Army continued to control the Holy City.

The Romans demonstrated their power. They crucified the Jewish King and thought that His claim of power was all over. His death seemed proof enough that the Messianic claims were false. "He was crucified, dead and buried." No one at this point in time considered the possibility of His Resurrection—not even His disciples!

The Messiah was killed with the full approval of the Jewish religious leaders in office. Religion and state had united to destroy the "King of the Jews." If God were to send a Messiah, could He have sent Him to a better place—to a more religious people? To a more expectant people, one that had clearly stated hopes of a Messiah? Yet Jesus failed to convince His own people, the Jews, of His claim to be God's Son. If He couldn't convince His own people, how could He be expected to convince an unbelieving Gentile world?

Christians must also be aware that they can be in danger of treating King Jesus with disrespectful familiarity. Many people get the false idea that if they have gone to church since they were children they know all there is to know about the Christian faith and the Bible and don't need to go to church anymore to be discipled. Some faithful church people may come to church now only out of habit, but they have long since lost their excitement and faith in Jesus. *Why?* Because they falsely think they know all there is to know about Him and imagine that they are doing all that Jesus would expect of them. Jesus has become too familiar, too predictable.

No use reading the Bible anymore; no surprises there, they think. If Jesus met rejection in His time from His own people, should Christians today be surprised if their efforts to share the faith and bring others into the Kingdom are frequently ignored? Maybe familiarity gets in the way again and the prophets are without honor in their own country. If Jesus, with His strengths, couldn't win everyone He met to His side, should Christians with weaknesses and imperfections expect to do better?

Maybe the painful lesson to be learned is that universal success in evangelism is not always possible as long as there is free will and choice. Jesus did not stop trying to reach people just because He was often met with rejection. Many of the Jews did become convinced believers and followed Him faithfully. The modern Church needs to be reminded of the rewards of persistence. For every failure to reach someone, some other person is eager to respond in faith.

Although Jesus promised his disciples that they would experience rejection, He also promised them that they would realize success. The promise of *success* should drive us on. Christ told us, ". . . if they kept my word, they will keep yours also" (John 15:20).

We will fail to persuade some. But others will respond to our efforts and invitations. Only persistent faithfulness can overcome the inertia that comes with the discouragement that is caused by rejection. Remember God's promises of success and reward, and continue sharing your faith with others.

> And let us not grow weary in well doing, for in due season we shall reap, if we do not lose heart. (Galatians 6:9)

> Be steadfast, unmovable, always abounding in the work of the Lord, knowing that in the Lord your labor is not in vain. (1 Corinthians 15:58)

Chapter Three

THE SAMARITANS

"And He sent messengers ahead of Him, who went and entered a village of the Samaritans, to make ready for Him; but the people would not receive Him, because His face was set toward Jerusalem."

—Luke 9:52–53

In Jesus' time the Samaritans and Jews were not on speaking terms with each other. Nursing ancient grudges, they in fact had a mutual contempt for each other. Each regarded the other as "untouchable." Jesus was in the middle. He wanted to reach out to both Jew and Samaritan, a mission unacceptable to either side. Jesus, the Jewish carpenter and teacher from Nazareth, looked past the label "Samaritan" and saw only people who needed Him in order that they might experience salvation. In His unique way, on one occasion He was successful in reaching some Samaritans.

Jesus approached a Samaritan woman at a well in Samaria. He asked her for a drink of water at a public place. Now, a Jewish man speaking to a Samaritan woman in a public place was an unthinkable act in that day. The woman herself was shocked at such daring defiance of acceptable custom and tradition. She questioned Jesus.

"How is it that you a Jew ask a drink of me, a woman of Samaria?" (John 4:9).

During the conversation that followed, the woman became convinced that Jesus must be a prophet because of His discernment of her unseemly past, as well as present liaisons. She listened as Jesus offered her spiritual "Living Water." She was so impressed that she told other Samaritan townspeople that Jesus was "the Savior of the World." Because of this woman's testimony, many became believers.

"Many Samaritans from that city believed in Him because of the woman's testimony" (John 4:39).

Because Jesus had time for *one* individual, many were touched by His concern and openness to non-Jewish people. With success like this, with one woman and her townspeople, it's no wonder that Jesus would readily want to enter other Samaritan towns seeking believers.

But success did not come everywhere. In another unnamed Samaritan town, Jesus was not welcomed by Samaritans. Jesus had sent messengers to announce His coming. That town made it very clear that Jesus was not welcome there. In fact, ". . . the people would not receive Him, because His face was set toward Jerusalem" (Luke 9:52–53).

The fact that He, being Jewish, was on His way to Jerusalem, where the Jewish Temple was located, offended their religious sensitivities. He was rejected by way of His association with that place. Samaritans refused to worship at Jerusalem. That was not *their* holy city. A long time ago Samaritans had begun to worship on Mount Gerizim at Sychar, present day Nablus. Mount Gerizim was *their* holy mount, not Mount Zion at Jerusalem. The woman at the well defended the Samaritan position on this issue:

Our fathers worshiped on this mountain; and you say that Jerusalem is where men ought to worship. (John 4:20)

The feud between the Jews and the Samaritans was an ancient quarrel over the rebuilding of the Temple after it had been destroyed by enemy forces. Samaritans were not allowed to help Jews in the reconstruction of it. The Samaritan town that Jesus now wanted to visit was being closed to His overtures because of this old feud.

This rejection was an embarrassment to Jesus' messengers. He would not be received with open arms in that place. No one there wanted to hear this Jewish carpenter. There would be no miracles or preaching of the Good News there.

Two disciples of Jesus, James and John, were appalled by the town's refusal to welcome Jesus. They saw this as an insult to the Master. Their "righteous anger" was directed squarely toward the disrespectful and inhospitable people. James and John reasoned that these Samaritan people should be honored that Jesus had selected their town to visit. Their faces must have flushed red with rage in light of its response.

James and John asked Jesus to give them His sanction and permission to destroy these ignorant people with fire from heaven. In *their* eyes, these inhospitable, ignorant people didn't deserve to live! This was grounds for a Holy War against unbelievers who didn't want to be saved. Such ingrates and infidels! James and John must have felt that the world would be a better place if such unbelievers were destroyed. This was their unloving plea to Jesus:

Lord, do you want us to bid fire to come down from heaven and consume them? (Luke 9:54)

After all, the prophet Elijah had done exactly this in the Old Testament. They were thus more than ready to imitate their hero of "the good old days." The attitude of these two early church leaders was, "No one is going to reject our Jesus and get away with it!" The hot-tempered apostles were willing to do the "dirty work" of fiery destruction. They didn't expect Jesus Himself to engage in the massacre. Their eagerness to call down fire from heaven does not sound too different than modern day world leaders who push for greater readiness to destroy millions of people in nuclear dust or by chemical and germ warfare—killing the nameless and faceless foreign enemies!

Jesus would certainly not grant their perverse request to firebomb the town. Dr. Luke's Gospel account says simply, "He turned and rebuked them" (Luke 9:55).

That sounds like the Jesus we know. How quickly Jesus' mission of love and salvation could have degenerated into a hate crusade, a holy war over religion. Instead, Jesus gave the direction to move on elsewhere: "And they went on to another village" (Luke 9:56).

Jesus offered the same advice to His followers as a mandate for all time. When we are rejected and unwelcome anywhere because of our faith, we are to move on to a more hospitable place, to another people.

> And if anyone will not receive you or listen to your words, shake off the dust from your feet as you leave that house or town. (Matthew 10:14)

It was a sad thing to see a whole town refuse revival and turn their backs on the salvation and healing that Jesus was offering them. They closed the door to Him, but their defiance did not mean that Jesus would then allow an unchristian crusade of death and destruction to be showered upon *them* by well-meaning disciples who could not understand His own unconditional love for the townspeople.

James and John were demonstrating *conditional* love. They would love these people *if* they welcomed Jesus. But since they refused to welcome Jesus, love was withdrawn instantly and replaced with vindictive rage. Conditional love is like that. History is full of examples of zealous religious people killing others in God's name if they were unreceptive to their particular viewpoints.

The Samaritans had no understanding of Jesus' mission. He was on His way to Jerusalem to die for them. He was trying to enter their town to offer them love, healing, and salvation. How could they have comprehended that? The old religious divisions of Jew and Samaritan blinded them from truth as old divisions and grievances have a way of doing everywhere, not just in the Middle East.

The "King of the Jews" was reaching out in love to Samaritans but they did not welcome His Jewish version of salvation. If they could have seen the loveless angry faces of James and John as a result of their inhospitality, they certainly would have misunderstood Christ's mission to them. Today many must also misunderstand the loving Christ because of unloving Christians who tragically misrepresent the real Jesus.

Who of us in Christ's church always exemplifies the spirit of Jesus for all people? If love is unconditional, it is constant—whether that love is accepted or not. Jesus was not about to stop loving people when they did not respond in faith. Even on the Cross, Jesus did not cry out for revenge on those who crucified Him. Instead, He prayed those very familiar words, "Father, forgive them, for they know not what they do" (Luke 23:34).

Today, Christians need to keep the love flowing unconditionally, as our Lord Jesus did.

The Bible reminds us that, ". . . while we were yet sinners Christ died for us" (Romans 5:8).

Theologians have called that "prevenient grace," God's gracious and amazing preceding love and offer of forgiveness by Christ's sacrifice on the cross for unmerited sinners in need of salvation.

Chapter Four

THE RICH MAN

"And Jesus looking upon him loved him, and said to him, 'You lack one thing; go, sell what you have, and give to the poor, and you will have treasure in heaven; and come, follow me.'"

—Mark 10:21–22

The story of the rich man walking away from Jesus exemplifies the reason why some people turn away from a church's efforts to evangelize them. The cost seems too great for them. The rich man was an honorable, religious person, yet he was holding on to something he regarded as more valuable than becoming a disciple of Jesus. He could not bring himself to surrender his prized possessions.

In calling upon him to surrender these, Jesus was hitting him in his most tender spot. His affluence was a stumbling block to Christian discipleship. Jesus was inviting him to become a disciple and a follower—an invitation that would clearly require *total* commitment.

Jesus could see how riches might stand in the way for this particular man. What if at some time later, perhaps in time of trial, he had to make a choice between wealth and faithful commitment to the Master? Which would he choose?

Jesus was challenging him to *consider the cost* at the beginning. How many would eagerly give up wealth and security for an uncertain, transcendent commitment to the Kingdom of God? Jesus did not go out looking for a rich man in particular. Jesus did not initiate the dialogue between Himself and the rich man. The rich man sought out Jesus to ask what would be required of him in order to be absolutely sure that he would have eternal life, boasting that he had been religiously and morally good throughout his lifetime.

Right from the start Jesus loved this man and wanted him to be his close follower. But Jesus pointed out one problem that needed correcting.

The rich man's assets would be only a liability if he were to follow Jesus. He could see that this man was holding on to his treasures for dear life. His possessions *possessed him*.

Riches don't always own a person, but as Christ could see, they did own this particular rich man. Because of what He saw, Jesus wanted him to "downsize" and give away his wealth to the needy. Without the excess baggage of wealth, he would someday enjoy treasures in heaven—a fair exchange for earthly wealth—and the honor of being a disciple of King Jesus.

The rich man wanted to know what would be required of him personally, and Jesus answered him. The answer was tough and uncompromising. Jesus loved him, and he would have made a good disciple. His generosity could have helped a lot of needy people right from the start of his entrance into discipleship, yet it wasn't to be.

Churches today have sometimes been accused of seeking out prosperous persons as prime targets for evangelism so they can support the church's financial needs and building programs and add to the church's prestige. A New Testament writer warned against Christians showing class or race distinctions or favoring the wealthy:

> For if a man with gold rings and in fine clothing comes into your assembly, and a poor man in shabby clothing also comes in, and you pay attention to the one who wears the fine clothing and say, "Have a seat here, please," while you say to the poor man, "Stand there," or "Sit at my feet," have you not made distinctions among yourselves, and become judges with evil thoughts? (James 2:2–4)

Did the rich man seek a challenge, or was he fishing for compliments from Jesus for the good that he claimed he had done? Jesus gave the man a difficult assignment. He would not now lower His expectations and bargain with him toward a "compromise solution." If he wanted to *do* something in order to have eternal life, as he'd indicated, then Jesus gave him his answer, stating *exactly* what he was to do.

The rich man did not come to Jesus acknowledging need or requesting mercy and forgiveness in order to obtain eternal life. Jesus only showed him what he lacked. Maybe someone should have advised the rich man, "Don't ask if you really don't want to know." Sometimes it's risky to ask a religious question.

Although the rich man had all the pleasures of this life to enjoy, he did not want to lose out on the happiness of heaven and the afterlife. Mark's Gospel describes this rich man running up to Jesus and kneeling at His feet. He was like a repentant sinner running up the sawdust trail at a revival meeting in response to an altar call by an evangelist offering salvation. He was ready to "do anything" to be assured of eternal life.

He was like an enthusiastic young person eager to know how to enter a challenging career. When his enthusiasm is tested, the candidate may think twice about the years of rigorous preparation and study that will be required of him.

When the rich man first asked what he should do to enter eternal life, Jesus responded quickly, reminding the rich man of the importance of obeying God's commandments.

"Do not kill, do not commit adultery, do not steal, do not bear false witness, do not defraud, honor your father and mother" (Mark 10:19). Jesus' reminder about obeying the commandments did not deter the enthusiastic inquirer. He confidently and proudly boasted that he had done all this from the time he was young.

"Teacher, all these I have observed from my youth," he said (Mark 10:20).

Jesus had no problem with that answer. He seemed pleased that a man could respond in this way. Such enthusiasm and religious zeal should not be discouraged, should it? *Or should it?* Jesus chose to test the rich man's response. He seemed to detect a weak spot in this particular seeker.

The rich man had one fault. Just one. The apostles must have been thinking at that moment, "Please, Jesus, don't chase him away. We *need* this man. Don't raise the requirements out of his reach. He's a good, religious man . . . and he's got money!"

Jesus told the man that his one fault could be corrected quickly, but it would be difficult. Jesus was not about to bargain over some compromise or water down truth in order to win a convert. Jesus did not prescribe the same requirement He gave another man by the name of Nicodemus when He told him, "You must be born anew" (John 3:7).

Instead, Jesus told the rich man he needed to sell his treasures and give the money to the poor.

Jesus was offering this man a place among the disciples. *What an honor!* But first, he would need to let go of something. Jesus saw plainly that the rich man was obsessed with accumulating wealth. That self-centeredness would block his future development of spiritual maturity and selfless concern for others. Until the rich man could let go of his possessions, he would not be prepared to follow Christ, whatever the cost.

The rich man's defense of his good, moral life was not enough to satisfy Jesus. He only *thought* he was ready to do anything for God. Like many people, he wanted to be religious, but on his own terms.

Many people today ask, "Can't you be a good Christian without going to church?" Many hope the pastor will be "Mr. Nice Guy" and give people an easy out rather than spell out the Lord's costly requirements of discipleship. No wonder many dislike "organized" religion.

All his life the rich man had spent accumulating wealth for himself. Now Jesus was asking him to give it away in a day. In exchange, Jesus offered him treasures in heaven. But why should he give up his secure investments so that others might benefit? The demands of Jesus seemed beyond all reason.

The scene resembled one of Jesus' parables—the stories that Jesus loved to tell to illustrate truth. In the parable, a merchant sold everything he had in order to acquire a particular, priceless pearl. For a moment it seemed like this rich man might imitate the merchant in the parable. The rich man was *so close* to the Kingdom, standing on the edge! But the cost made him back down. His enthusiasm waned, and he just walked away from Jesus, sadly.

The stakes were too high, and the rich man couldn't gamble away *all* he had for an uncertain return on his investment. The apostles must have wondered why Jesus didn't just ask the rich man to give a tithe. That would be better than nothing, wouldn't it?

Why couldn't Jesus have just challenged the rich man to help build the first Christian church in Jerusalem? Why didn't Jesus just encourage this man to continue doing good and following God's commandments? Why did he need to get rid of *all* of his wealth by giving it away? If Jesus could only have been a good compromiser He might have gained another follower—a rich one at that.

But Jesus knew what He was doing. He was making a *great* offer. He was inviting the rich man into His inner circle. He was offering him a chance to follow the Christ, a chance to become an apostle. Jesus was giving the rich man something spectacular in exchange for a sacrifice—discipleship on earth and treasure in another dimension, in heaven!

The rich man walked away, and we don't even know his name. The nameless man had been given a chance to see Jesus in action daily, to watch Him perform miraculous healings, to hear Him teach before spellbound audiences. He had the chance to see the risen Christ appear before His followers.

Had he chosen, he might have been a daily companion of men like Peter, James, John, and the other disciples. His name would have been added in the Bible beside the names of men who were part of salvation "history in the making." Instead, he declined Jesus' invitation to discipleship and simply walked away. He would miss out on the adventure of a lifetime. But he could keep his wealth and was free to accumulate more.

It was his choice, although the one he made—to do nothing—seems like a sad one. ". . . And he went away sorrowful; for he had great possessions." (Mark 10:22).

Jesus failed to win this man. This one got away. Don't many people turn away from church today for fear of what demands the church might put on them?

Many today are afraid of making a commitment to Christ. Something seems to hold them back. People seem to fear Jesus' call to discipleship because of what they might have to give up, and it's not just money. It might be grudges, rage, pride, racism, hate, comforts, time, self-pity, an addiction, some moral deviation or their deep-seated indifference to human suffering.

As the rich man walked away, Jesus shared a lesson with His disciples. He told them, "How hard it will be for those who have riches to enter the kingdom of God. It is easier for a camel to go through the eye of a needle than for a rich man to enter the kingdom of God" (Mark 10:24–25).

Many, even in Jesus' time, saw prosperity as a sign that God's favor was on a person. Wasn't prosperity a sign of wise investing, shrewdness, thrift, industry, and self-discipline? Wealth gets immediate respect and courtesy. Who wouldn't like being pampered with fine dining, rooms in the best hotels, and riding in luxury chariots and boats? If one gave it all away, what would there be to do or talk about?

A wealthy person can talk almost endlessly about investments, the stock market, interest rates, the gold market, real estate values, antiques, tax shelters, precious gems, fine art, and compound interest. All else might sound dull to a person so preoccupied with wealth and its protection. Hadn't Jesus once reminded His followers that one's heart followed one's treasure?

"For where your treasure is, there will be your heart also," the Lord had said (Matthew 6:21). Our story ends sadly. The rich man was not an enemy. Jesus lost a good man, a moral man. He lost someone the Bible says he *loved*.

The rich man had a lack. Don't we all? In fact, the one fault we all have, according to Scripture, is that we are all sinners in need of forgiveness and salvation. That doesn't stop Jesus from reaching out to touch us and invite us into His Kingdom. Jesus wants to make up for our lack. Salvation is by grace, not by anything *we* do.

Christ invites us to follow Him. He doesn't force discipleship on anyone, anymore than He did upon the rich man. Christ always leaves room for the individual to reject the invitation. He honors free, personal choice and gives us the opportunity to walk away.

Love and grace are offered freely, not forcibly. Jesus doesn't force His way into a person's life uninvited. According to the Bible, He stands at the door of a person's heart and knocks. The choice is now up to the hearer.

> Behold, I stand at the door and knock; if anyone hears my voice and opens the door, I will come in to him and eat with him, and he with me. (Revelation 3:20)

How many gifted young people have rejected Christ's call to some form of Christian ministry because they were enticed into another career that promised greater financial rewards? I thank God for the high honor and privilege of being called into His ministry. I am thankful now that I didn't choose something else, although many times over the years, during stressful times in particular, I questioned the wisdom of continuing my calling.

Chapter Five

HYPOCRITES—BLIND GUIDES

"Woe to you, scribes and Pharisees, hypocrites! Woe to you, blind guides . . ."
— *Jesus Christ, Matthew 23:16*

Look who Jesus dared to call hypocrites—the religious elite of the community. He dared to confront Pharisees and Scribes, God's defenders and interpreters of the Mosaic Law. No one likes to be labeled a hypocrite, *especially* religious leaders. They quickly accused Jesus of blasphemy—of heresy!

He counter-charged with accusations of hypocrisy. Note that Jesus' accusers never charged Jesus with hypocrisy. They never accused Jesus of teaching one thing and doing another. How could they? His life matched His teaching. They also never charged Jesus with being self-righteous, even though He stood openly in judgment of His accusers.

If anybody made Jesus angry, it was the religious leaders of His time. His wrath was not focused on the *secular* culture or even on *political* leaders, but on the *religious* community. *Why?* He may have felt that the religious community should be setting a credible example of faith in God for the secular culture around it.

Jesus became very angry and confrontational with religious leaders who were supposed to be setting a moral example, but were not living up to their own precepts. Jesus called these pious men uncomplimentary names like *blind fools, serpents, brood of vipers, a child of hell, blind guides and hypocrites.* Now how do you suppose these Scribes and Pharisees would respond to such accusations?

Jesus would not be popular with religious dignitaries, who wanted to defend their honor in the community. The Scripture points out that they were out to get Him—hoping that He would say something that they could use as condemning evidence against Him.

Religious leaders became Jesus' enemies. No one was going to accuse these community leaders of being hypocrites and get away with it.

> As He went away from there, the scribes and the Pharisees began to press him hard, and to provoke him to speak of many things, lying in wait for Him, to catch him at something He might say. (Luke 11:53–54)

Jesus could not stand hypocrisy, obviously. He was harder on religious hypocrites than He was on immoral sinners, on thieves, on tax collectors, on political leaders, or on oppressors, all whom would have had bad reputations in the eyes of the religious community.

Religious people, in particular, can make very legalistic and moralistic judgments of others. These sins of pride and self-righteousness were traits that Jesus confronted head on. He accused the Pharisees of playacting, of outwardly appearing to be what they actually were not. That is hypocrisy, to teach one thing and do another.

Such false appearance of virtue was a stench for Jesus. But hypocrites can be very convinced of their own rightness and goodness. Hypocrites can have a very short memory and become blind to their own imperfections and moral failures of thought, of word, and of deed. They quickly point out the faults of others while failing to even see their own.

The prophet Isaiah, speaking for God, said it well centuries ago: "This people honors me with their lips, but their heart is far from me" (Isaiah 29:13). Jesus knew the hearts of people and their imperfections. He could see behind their masks.

The Pharisees and Scribes once brought a woman to Him who had been caught in the very act of adultery to see what moral judgment Jesus would make on her. In the religious culture of that time, they reminded Jesus that Moses had directed that such a person should die by stoning. That is a harsh punishment for adultery. The religion of Islam today still defends such a harsh punishment for this sin.

Jesus watched the religious men standing there, like unforgiving sexist executioners, feeling so superior and self-righteous over this poor woman that they wanted stoned. Only the woman was brought for judgment, not the man, who had also been involved. Her judges wanted to see if Jesus would share their harsh infliction of punishment or whether He would back off the religious directive of Moses and face condemnation Himself as condoning immorality.

The religious leaders present were relishing their pious, religious position. They figured now that they had Jesus in a corner, asking Him for His opinion about whether stoning was appropriate or not. But Jesus saw through their playacting. He knew how men thought, how they talked, and how they behaved. But He called their bluff. What was His challenge to anyone who claimed to be sinless?

"Let him who is without sin among you be the first to throw a stone at her" (John 8:7).

Not one of the religious leaders dared to claim that he was sinless, thus qualified to throw the first stone. One by one, each sheepishly slipped away, until not one accuser was left. Jesus then spoke words of forgiveness to the woman and gave her a directive for the future. "Neither do I condemn you; go and do not sin again" (John 8:11).

The woman who had been caught in the act of adultery walked away freely, unharmed. There were no accusers left to condemn her. Jesus had seen through the hypocrisy of the religious leaders, and they knew it. The harsh judges realized they had been judged and it was humiliating. The woman had found a friend and an advocate in Jesus. She was able to walk away with a clean slate. She was free to start over again. Jesus *did* want to keep her out of future adulterous relationships. The past was over and done, forgiven. He told her not to repeat her sin again.

Self-righteous people are the hardest people to change. They are convinced that they have arrived and that others are far behind them. They have convinced themselves that they are right. Judging people is easy for the self-righteous and it becomes a daily habit for many religious people. True *self*-examination becomes nearly impossible for these unless condemning evidence is overwhelming and indisputable. Even then, they can be blind to their heart-error.

The Pharisees would continue pointing their condemning fingers at Jesus, looking for something He would say or do that they could use to destroy His reputation and His continued threat to their authority. How many leaders of World Religions today would be just as hard to convert?

Jesus not only accused the religious leaders of being hypocrites. He also said that these leaders were *blind fools, blind guides*. That's not very complimentary to men who *thought* they could see religious truth better than anyone else. Jesus told them they were living in darkness, like blind men. They would naturally take this as an insult.

Pious people often believe that they know it all and have closed minds. They can be the hardest type of people to convince otherwise. As the old saying goes, "Don't confuse me with the facts; my mind is already made up."

Jesus would probably describe a lot of today's leaders of *all* World Religions as blind and hypocritical. He would make a lot of people today angry with His denunciation of world leaders who can't see the truth beyond their own mistaken preconceived perceptions.

Jesus was referring to spiritual blindness when He said that the religious leaders of His day were *blind guides*. They had physical vision. They could see, yet they were blind. Jesus once said that this was why He used parables to teach. These religious leaders could listen to His stories, but they could not see the point Jesus was making, because they were spiritually blind.

> This is why I speak to them in parables, because seeing they do not see and hearing they do not hear, nor do they understand. (Matthew 13:13)

Paul, in one of his letters, described spiritual blindness, saying, "The unspiritual man does not receive the gifts of the Spirit of God, for they are folly to him, and he is not able to understand them because they are spiritually discerned" (1 Corinthians 2:14). Another letter in the New Testament also describes spiritual blindness as a state that occurs when one hates others:

"But he who hates his brother is in the darkness and walks in the darkness, and does not know where he is going, because the darkness has blinded his eyes" (1 John 2:11).

Even in today's world, there are religious leaders who teach their followers to hate—even to kill.

Jesus knew that religious leaders who defend God and His laws are not exempt from spiritual blindness. The prophet Isaiah had many years before described God's frustration with the messengers and servants He had sent to the people.

> Who is blind but my servant, or deaf as my messenger whom I send? Who is blind as my dedicated one, or blind as the servant of the Lord? He sees many things but does not observe them; his ears are open, but he does not hear. (Isaiah 42:19–20)

Nonreligious people aren't the only ones who can be spiritually blind. So are many of the Lord's committed people! Converts like John Newton, who wrote *Amazing Grace* in 1779, readily admitted his previous blindness during a time when he was deeply involved in the slave trade. He described this blindness in the words of his immortal hymn, saying, "I once was lost, but now am found; was blind, but now I see."

People are spiritually blind when they don't see wrongs and injustices, when they don't see needy and hurting people, when they don't recognize truth, when they can't see their own flaws, when they continue in ignorance and hate, when they don't appreciate their blessings, when they don't understand what God is trying to tell them, when they don't understand how much God loves them and when they mock the truth that Jesus was sent by God to save this world.

It is terrible to lose one's eyesight. It is also terrible to be spiritually blind. Today, for those who will receive it, Jesus gives sight to the spiritually blind, just as He restored sight to many who were physically blind during His earthly ministry. If we were honest, we would have to confess that we *all* have a blind spot somewhere. Let's not reject blindly our Lord's great offer of healing!

Chapter Six

LEADERS OF RELIGION AND GOVERNMENT

"The Son of man must suffer many things and be rejected by the elders and chief priests and scribes, and be killed, and on the third day be raised."

—Luke 9:22

In the words of the Apostle's Creed, Jesus Christ "suffered under Pontius Pilate." Leaders of Temple and State, religious leaders and government leaders, in an unholy alliance, jointly resisted Jesus and condemned Him to death by public crucifixion as an accused enemy of the people.

Secular governments and dictatorships, as well as governments under religious control, *still* try to silence alternative religious expression, such as Christian evangelism. Often in history, organized religion, even Christianity, has tried to forcefully stamp out religious differences. Powerful religious forces, aligned with the power and authority of government, have outlawed minority religious expression by force—and sometimes even by death.

It may come as no surprise that the Christian church suffered mass persecution under secular Communism or that ancient Christians suffered terribly under the persecution of the Roman Empire. But the Church has also suffered greatly in religious nations controlled by world religions in which Christian evangelism is not welcome. So, is what happened in Christ's day really so incredible?

In the biblical account of the Crucifixion, both religious leaders and government leaders gave their approval to the murder of Jesus Christ. Jesus failed to win the support of the leaders in power—both religious and state. Sadly, as church history reminds us, even Christians themselves have persecuted other Christians who have differing opinions and convictions. Religious zeal, Christian or non-Christian, can evolve into terrible cruelty and intolerance in any century.

It was one thing for Jesus to see completely secular Gentile unbelievers resist His teaching. It was another for Jesus to be called a *blasphemer* by the chief Jewish priests, who believed in God and in the Torah. Jesus warned His followers that they too would be put to death by conscientious, God-fearing people.

"Indeed, the hour is coming when whoever kills you will think he is offering service to God" (John 16:2).

Can organized religion ever pose such a threat to true believers? It must have sounded incredible to the apostles that religious people could think that they were doing God a favor by killing the followers of Jesus Christ. The high priest accused Jesus of blasphemy when Jesus told him that He not only was the Son of God and the Christ but that He would someday be seen "sitting at the right hand of Power" and would come back to earth in the clouds of heaven.

What a claim to make before the head of a powerful, organized religion! If Jesus failed to convince religious leaders like Annas and Caiaphas of His Lordship, one should not be surprised to see Jesus failing to reach the leaders of secular government like Pilate and Herod.

It took the united efforts of organized religion and state, of Jews and Gentiles, to authorize the Crucifixion. Any Gentile who wants to blame the Crucifixion totally on the Jews is ignorant and wrong, conveniently forgetting that the actual torture and death of Jesus on the Cross was done physically by Gentile soldiers and ordered by a Gentile governor, Pontius Pilate, who represented the justice system of the Roman Empire and the will of the people. In fact, Jesus had predicted that His death would be inflicted by Gentiles!

> For He will be delivered to the Gentiles, and will be mocked, and shamefully treated and spit upon; they will scourge Him and will kill Him, and on the third day He will rise. (Luke 18:32–33)

Why couldn't it have been different? Why couldn't religious leaders, of all people, recognize that the Messiah had arrived in their midst? Jesus saw it all coming; He saw religious leaders rejecting His claims and clamoring for His death. Jesus could feel the hostility building.

Peter tried to restrain Jesus' intention to walk right into the city of Jerusalem, where He himself had predicted He would face opposition and death at the direction of the chief priests and elders. But Jesus would not allow Himself to be deterred from doing what He knew He must do.

These religious leaders wouldn't stop with criticism and ostracism. They wanted *blood*. And they got it. But they needed the secular power of the reigning Roman government to authorize the death of Jesus. The State ultimately held the power of life and death.

The High Priest was convinced that Jesus was a bad influence on the religious community and that He should be destroyed in order to preserve the true faith.

The religious leaders were sensitive about power. Jesus was a threat to their authority over the people. Jesus talked freely and boldly about His power before the High Priest, saying, "But I tell you, hereafter you will see the Son of man seated at the right hand of power, and coming on the clouds of Heaven" (Matthew 26:64)

The threat of Jesus' growing popularity and power over the people was of great concern to the religious leaders. Many Jews believed in Jesus after they saw Him bring a dead man back from the grave. That dead man was Lazarus, a close friend of Jesus. The priests and Pharisees convened a council.

At the council meeting the religious leaders wondered what they should do in response to this worker of many signs. "If we let Him go on thus, everyone will believe in Him, and the Romans will come and destroy both our holy place and our nation," they said among themselves (John 11:48).

They feared Jesus might lead an uprising of the people that would be crushed by the Romans, along with the whole religious establishment. Caiaphas, the High Priest, made a remark at the council meeting to the effect that *it's better that one person die than for a nation to die.* That one person would be Jesus.

> You do not understand that it is expedient for you that one man should die for the people, and that the whole nation should not perish. (High Priest Caiaphas) (John 11:50)

But the religious leaders still had a problem. They did not have the authority to order Jesus' death for blasphemy. The authority was definitely in the hands of the State, the Roman governmental justice system. Pilate and Herod represented that authority.

Pilate could not be counted on to stand courageously for the right even he could see and understand. Herod saw the whole matter as a joke and handed it all back to Pilate. Pilate, under public pressure demanding crucifixion, politically caved in and washed his hands of the matter, turning Jesus over for execution.

If Jesus could not find an ally in the religious establishment, neither could He find an ally in government leaders. Neither Temple nor State would grant sanctuary for "the King of the Jews." Jesus was a rejected outcast, alone and vulnerable. "He was despised and rejected by men; a man of sorrows, and acquainted with grief; and as one from whom men hide their faces; he was despised, and we esteemed him not" (Isaiah 53:3).

The religious leaders then stirred up the crowds, getting them to loudly demand the Crucifixion of this self-proclaimed Messiah. No one stood up for Jesus. No one pleaded on His behalf. There were no outcries of support for the Christ. By the will of the people a criminal by the name of Barabbas was released rather than Jesus.

Pilate was the representative of the State who took responsibility for ordering the whipping of Jesus, as well as His Crucifixion. The infamous name of the Gentile governor is repeated over and over by Christians every time they affirm their faith with the Apostles' Creed and the Nicene Creed. He [Jesus] ". . . suffered under Pontius Pilate, was crucified, dead, and buried" (The Apostles' Creed).

Note that no mention is made in these creeds of the esteemed religious leaders Annas and Caiaphas, who were acting on their zealous, conscientious convictions to defend the faith and the people. They were sincere, God-fearing men. They just did not believe Jesus' claims.

World leaders of religion and government today still exert great influence and control over the people they lead and govern. That powerful and authoritative influence can be a formidable obstacle to evangelism.

Jesus looked with futility into the eyes of leaders of religion and government for support. All He must have seen from Herod and Pilate were icy, cold, cynical stares devoid of understanding and heated rage in the glaring eyes of Annas and Caiaphas. Pilate's order for Jesus' Crucifixion was a cold, impersonal sentence, an order for soldiers to obey and carry out at his command.

The bureaucracy made an unjust judgment that God would ultimately use to save a lost and dying world. Jesus was unable to reach the leaders of religion and government of His day, so then His death would bypass them and bring salvation to the world directly. Jesus said it well, "And I, when I am lifted up from the earth, will draw all men to myself" (John 12:32).

Christ's power was not diminished or destroyed by a cross. He had power on the Cross as well as in His glorious resurrection. God would turn around the bad decisions of foolish leaders of the people and use their folly for good. Even today, Jesus may still fail to reach the proud leaders of religion or government. He may still fail to reach the mighty in power, the rich and famous, the respected, or the educated leaders of society who defiantly refuse to submit to Christ's authority over them, who refuse to bow to the King. That is nothing new. The Psalmist said it centuries ago:

The kings of the earth set themselves, and the rulers take counsel together, against the Lord and His anointed. (Psalm 2:2)

King Jesus does not ultimately fail. People can ignore Him and defy Him all they want, but like it or not, there will come a time when *all* will have to submit to Him.

Therefore God has highly exalted Him and bestowed on Him the name which is above every name, that at the name of Jesus every knee should bow, in heaven and on earth and under the earth, and every tongue confess that Jesus Christ is Lord, to the glory of God the Father. (Philippians 2:9–11)

When the Son of man comes in His glory, and all the angels with Him, then He will sit on His glorious throne. (Matthew 25:31)

King Jesus will have the final word. Leaders and rulers will someday have to give an account to the King of Kings and Lord of Lords. Judgment Day is coming—a day of humbling for the proud and mighty.

Admittedly, it is hard for an important religious or secular leader who is used to giving orders to submit to the orders of another and to listen as a disciple, a servant. What can turn proud, self-righteous, successful, rich leaders into humble disciples of Christ, ready to learn and obey? Nothing short of a miracle can do it.

Leaders in any field can be the hardest to reach because of their prestigious positions and powerful egos. Nevertheless, "with God, all things are possible."

Chapter Seven

SATAN, "THE DEVIL"

"And Jesus, full of the Holy Spirit, returned from the Jordan, and was led by the Spirit for forty days in the wilderness, tempted by the devil."

—Luke 4:1–2

At the start of Jesus' ministry He was confronted by Satan's cunning and enticing appeals. According to Scripture, the Spirit led Jesus out into a wilderness area, a stony and barren, mountainous place. He ate no food for forty days. It was here that Satan tried to win Jesus over. This is the one place in Scripture where Jesus engaged in a debate with Satan, His arch-enemy. The debate ended in a stalemate, neither convincing the other.

The forty days of Lent recall the forty days Jesus spent fasting in the wilderness debating Satan over three temptations. Jesus' "Spring Training Program" for the Cross would be a spiritual pilgrimage and retreat in the wilderness, a time for defining His role as Savior, engaging in prayer, radical self-discipline, and reflection. Satan tried to persuade Jesus to build His kingdom Satan's way instead of God's way.

Some people don't believe that Satan is real, but rather a demonic force personified only in people who yield to their baser instincts. But Jesus knew Satan was real and personal—the chief of demons. No one had to persuade Jesus that Satan was real.

The Satan-connection on planet earth is not well understood by the unperceptive. Only the spiritually discerning can see the connection. The unperceptive see only solitary sources of evil acting on their own. They fail to see the very real *conspiracy* against God orchestrated by Satan.

Satan approached God's Son at the very beginning of His ministry, trying to sway Jesus from His mission with three enticing temptations. First, Satan told Jesus to use His power as the Son of God to turn stones into bread in order to satisfy His own hunger there in the wilderness. Secondly, Satan told Jesus to worship *him* in exchange for political power as ruler of all the nations of the world.

Thirdly, Satan told Jesus He should put God's promises of protection by angels to the test by jumping off the highest part of the sacred Temple in Jerusalem. Satan very cleverly quoted Scripture in his enticing temptations, trying to catch the Son of God off guard.

Satan quoted this biblical promise from one of the Psalms, "For He will give His angels charge over you to guard you in all your ways. On their hands they will bear you up, lest you dash your foot against a stone" (Psalm 91:11–12).

Such piety could confuse many a gullible believer, but Jesus was too knowledgeable of Scripture for that to happen and too wise to be deceived by the cunning manipulator. Jesus quoted Scripture in each of His responses to the three temptations. He refuted the Tempter with God's answer, God's Word. These were the scriptures Jesus quoted:

It is written, "Man shall not live by bread alone."
(Deuteronomy 8:3)

It is written, "You shall worship the Lord your God, and
Him only shall you serve." (Deuteronomy 6:13)

It is said, "You shall not tempt the Lord your God."
(Deuteronomy 6:16)

Satan tried to get Jesus to compromise. Satan wasn't
about to be persuaded by the Bible-quoting, uncompromising, Messianic King, At the end of the story, Luke implies
that Satan will be back later when he says, "And when the
devil had ended every temptation, he departed from Him
until an opportune time" (Luke 4:13).

This encounter was not the end of Satan. It had been
not only a battle of words, but also a battle of very strong,
unchangeable wills. The battle lines had been drawn. The
great battle between these two would not ultimately be won
by debate or by argument. Jesus and Satan understood each
other ever since their encounter in the wilderness. The con-
flict would only get more intense as Jesus attacked Satan's
strongholds.

Offering three temptations, Satan had looked for weaknesses in God's Son, areas where Jesus might be persuaded
to compromise the mission God had sent Him to complete.
Jesus could see what a master strategist and deceiver Satan
was, who could disguise himself to appear as an "angel of
light," as Paul once described the devil (2 Corinthians 11:14).

Jesus now began His three-year ministry of loving words
and deeds, of preaching and teaching, accompanied by awe-
some, miraculous signs. Jesus had determined that He
would not use His God-given power and authority as the
Son of God for self-serving purposes, like turning rocks
into a meal for Himself, even when he was intensely hungry.

He could easily have done so. Neither would Christ put God's promises to the test in order to impress people by jumping off high stone walls.

Jesus would forego Satan's invitation to a show of political, military, and financial power in order to gain followers and admirers. He chose, rather, to use His power to heal the sick people who'd been stricken by Satan. He would free people who had been bound and possessed by Satan. He would offer salvation to sinners burdened down with guilt. He offered love to the friendless and the shunned.

In fact, Jesus was always undoing the destructive evil work of Satan, the adversary of God and man. When Jesus saw His own disciples experiencing victories over demons, He knew that he was victorious and cried out, "I saw Satan fall like lightening from heaven" (Luke 10:18).

Every time Jesus healed or saved a person, He won a victory over Satan's captive power. Truly, there was a war going on between God's Son and the fallen angel. Jesus would only provoke Satan's hatred and anger all the more as He was healing what Satan had destroyed.

Jesus was undoing Satan's villainous work, but Satan was not about to give up his power willingly. Wickedness is not noted for conceding easily. If Satan were to be unseated, God would have to use a strategy that would catch Satan off guard.

Jesus' three-year ministry did not bring healing and salvation to every needy person worldwide. In fact, as we know all too well, Satan's power and influence are still very evident worldwide twenty centuries later. Just read the newspaper and listen to the evening news—you'll find ample evidence of Satan's destructive activities.

Incredibly, Jesus was once accused by a Pharisee of possessing demonic power because He was casting out demons. But everything Christ did revealed how ridiculous this accusation truly was. In fact, He was constantly casting out demons and undoing Satan's work of destruction by bringing healing and restoration. Jesus said that casting out demons and healing was a sign of God's Kingdom, not a sign of some demonic power! "But if it is by the finger of God that I cast out demons, then the kingdom of God has come upon you," He said (Luke 11:20).

God's strategy that would end Satan's rule on earth sounded like a doomed one. Jesus talked about how He would have to suffer and die in order to fulfill His God-sent mission. "The Son of man must suffer many things and be rejected by the elders and chief priests and scribes, and be killed, and on the third day be raised" (Luke 9:22).

How could this be a *success* strategy? Even His closest disciples didn't hear the part that He would be resurrected on the third day. They only focused on the part that predicted His suffering and dying. The Battle Plan sounded awful. When Jesus talked about this plan, Peter once scolded Him for saying such a thing. "God forbid, Lord! This shall never happen to you," he exclaimed (Matthew 16:22).

Jesus reprimanded Peter for trying to stop Him from going through with the plan with these words, "Get behind me, Satan! You are a hindrance to me; for you are not on the side of God, but of men" (Matthew 16:23). Jesus would not compromise God's plan in exchange for Satan's tempting alternative just to avoid suffering and death, as Peter had suggested.

The disciples wanted nothing less than a "success strategy" from their Messiah. If Jesus was unable to win Satan, He must certainly not allow Himself to be rejected and killed by others if He was going to achieve victory over Satan's rule and power.

But the plan of history could not be changed. God's strategy prevailed and the Messianic King entered Jerusalem on a lowly donkey rather than on a white, triumphant horse signifying victorious royalty. This was the beginning of a week that led up to the cross.

All during His three-year ministry of word and deed Jesus failed to change Satan, who remained unrepentant and unrelenting. Satan wasn't impressed with Jesus' ministry of love, healing, and forgiveness. He didn't want to be saved and would remain Jesus' greatest enemy. Satan was unmoved by Jesus' eloquent sermons and teaching, His profound parables, and His invitations to discipleship.

Satan would never respond to any call of the Lord. Jesus and Satan were at *war* with each other. Satan had his strategies; Jesus had His. The devil, like Jesus' own disciples, must have been perplexed by the paradoxical nature of his enemy's battle plan. *How could Jesus' strategy win by becoming vulnerable to crucifixion? How can one succeed by losing? How can one live by dying? How can one be strong by appearing weak? How can a dead King on a cross ever rise up again in victory?*

God's strange strategy would catch Satan completely off guard. Paul said it so well: "For the foolishness of God is wiser than men, and the weakness of God is stronger than men" (1 Corinthians 1:25).

Jesus knew His followers would be involved in the battle as well. The writer of the New Testament letter to the Church at Ephesus reminds believers of the *spiritual* battle ahead. "Put on the whole armor of God, that you may be able to stand against the wiles of the devil . . ." (Ephesians 6:11).

During Jesus' ministry, Satan realized that he could not control the Son of God. If Satan couldn't stop Jesus, he would infiltrate Jesus' followers—a devious strategy that Satan still tries to carry out today.

Satan decided to enter the inner circle of Jesus' select twelve apostles. If Jesus would not compromise, Satan would look for a compromising apostle who would, for a price, cooperate as an accomplice in a conspiracy to neutralize Jesus' claims. He tried this with Judas, then with Peter.

Jesus knew that Satan had his sights set on Peter. Jesus told Peter that He had been praying for him because of Satan's intent. "Simon, Simon, Satan demanded to have you, that he might sift you like wheat, but I have prayed for you that your faith may not fail" (Luke 22:31–32). Only Jesus' prayer could save Peter. Yet even so, Peter still denied three times that he was a follower of Jesus, just as Jesus had predicted.

Judas, the group's trusted treasurer, was the one disciple who *could* be totally won to Satan's control. Judas had a weak spot that could be compromised: his love of money. Thirty pieces of silver was all that was necessary to persuade him to betray his master. For a price, Judas Iscariot would do Satan's beckoning. Here was a follower of Jesus who could bend principle, then offer the kiss of betrayal.

Luke's Gospel says that Satan entered into Judas and gained total control of him. What Satan directed, Judas would do. Satan could never get this kind of control over Jesus, so he targeted one whom Jesus loved.

> Then Satan entered into Judas Iscariot, who was of the number of the twelve; he went away and conferred with the chief priests and officers how he might betray Him to them. (Luke 22:3–4)

Satan was done debating with Jesus. He would now use Judas to bring Jesus to trial and death. Satan would set things in motion for the Crucifixion. Earlier in His ministry Jesus had told some religious leaders that they were being used by Satan—an unthinkable concept in their view!

> You are of your father the devil . . . He was a murderer from the beginning, and has nothing to do with the truth because there is no truth in him. When he lies, he speaks

according to his own nature, for he is a liar and the father of lies. (John 8:44)

Jesus was unable to reach this incorrigible enemy. Human beings could be evangelized, but Satan was unchangeable and heartless, hateful, defiant, and deceitful to the end. Satan was one enemy even Jesus could not love. Satan was trying to destroy everyone Jesus loved and desired to save. Now Satan was designing a plan and strategy that would backfire into becoming part of God's plan of salvation to redeem a world of sinners.

It began the night Jesus was betrayed by Judas and was arrested in the garden outside Jerusalem. Before going into the garden, Jesus celebrated Passover with His disciples. He sensed what would happen that night and wanted to prepare His disciples. He offered them bread and the cup of Passover wine in the Upper Room in order to remind them of His approaching death. They were to remember His death, and as often as they did so to proclaim that His body was offered as atonement for sin.

Satan was at work orchestrating people to betray and falsely accuse Jesus as well as to arouse crowds to demand crucifixion for his arch-enemy, God's Son. Strange as it may seem, God let it all happen in order to achieve a greater good, an ultimate victory. As His Son willingly submitted Himself to the humiliation and terrible awfulness of the Cross, it soon became clear that Jesus was not going down in defeat, as it may at first have appeared.

The hymn writer Reginald Heber got it right when, he wrote, "The Son of God goes forth to war, a kingly crown to gain."

As Jesus carried His Cross through the city streets of Jerusalem, He was going to war nonviolently. For the three hours He agonized on the Cross, Jesus was *at war.* Then the war ended and Jesus shouted *Victory!* "It is finished" (John 19:30). With Jesus' death, the war only *appeared* to be lost. Christ's glorious Resurrection would change all that. Christ could never again be killed. Within three days, He was back and alive forevermore!

Satan's days are numbered; his power doomed. To side with Satan from then on would be to side with a *losing cause.* Christ would be the victorious King. Satan would still continue trying to implement his cruel design, knowing his days are numbered. "But woe to you, O earth and sea, for the devil has come down to you in great wrath, because he knows that his time is short" (Revelation 12:12). In the end, God would have the final victory.

People now have a way out of Satan's control. They can yield themselves to Christ's control and declare themselves to be under His Lordship. Christ offers salvation, healing, and eternal life. Satan can't take away the treasures in heaven. Notably absent in the resurrection life of God's Kingdom of heaven will be Christ's archenemy, Satan. No longer will the roaring lion (1 Peter 5:8) be a threat to God's people. Another Lion will rule—the Lion of Judah, Jesus Christ.

> Weep not; lo, the Lion of the tribe of Judah, the root of David, has conquered. (Revelation 5:5)

Even Jesus could not convert Satan. The Scriptures quite graphically describe Satan's end.

> And then the lawless one will be revealed, and the Lord Jesus shall slay him with the breath of His mouth and destroy him by His appearing and His coming. (2 Thessalonians 2:8)

> And the devil who had deceived them was thrown into the lake of fire and sulphur where the beast and the false

prophet live. And they will be tormented day and night forever and ever. (Revelation 20:10)

The Devil looks big and grim and seemingly indestructible, until we see that it's all over for him when King Jesus stands in victory. Martin Luther, the great Protestant reformer, said it ever so well in his famous hymn, "A Mighty Fortress Is Our God."

> For still our ancient foe doth seek to work us woe;
> His craft and power are great, and armed with cruel hate,
> on earth is not his equal.

> The Prince of Darkness grim, we tremble not for him;
> his rage we can endure, for lo, his doom is sure;
> one little word shall fell him.

Satan's end is certain because one little Word shall fell him: *Jesus*. Victory belongs to our God and to His Son, King Jesus. Satan has lost the war! Jesus will be King over a greater Kingdom than any that history has known—an *eternal* Kingdom of justice and truth, a Kingdom of peace and love— the Kingdom of God.

> Then comes the end, when He delivers the kingdom to God the Father after destroying every rule and every authority and power. For He must reign until He has put all His enemies under His feet. The last enemy to be destroyed is death. (1 Corinthians 15:24–26)

Chapter Eight

JUDAS ISCARIOT

"Truly, I say to you, one of you will betray me."
                                        —Matthew 26:21

*"Then Satan entered into Judas called Iscariot, who was of
the number of the twelve; he went away and conferred with
the chief priests and officers how he might betray Him to
them."*
                                        —Luke 22:3–4

The first Communion supper was held in the up-
stairs of a private home, not in a church or synagogue. An upper room served as a dining room for the special Passover meal for Jesus and His inner circle of disciples.

Jesus had handpicked the place beforehand—a place
unknown to the disciples. Jesus told Peter and John to look
for a man carrying a container of water who would meet
and guide them. They were to follow the man to a house.
When they got there, they were to ask where the room was
where the teacher would eat Passover dinner with His

disciples. A dining room became transformed into a sacred place for this intimate gathering before the Cross.

In March of 1982 I had the privilege of touring the Holy Land and visited the traditional site of the Upper Room in Jerusalem with twelve other pastors and our guides. I will never in my lifetime forget climbing up the outer steps to the Upper Room with those pastors on that spiritual pilgrimage.

These were the same pastors I had just been joking with on the bus. Here we were, climbing the stairs to an upper room—like the apostles of old, repeating history. It was a strange feeling to think what it must have been like to have been with the apostles and the Lord Jesus Christ for the Passover meal on that momentous night or to receive the first Communion Sacrament.

During the three years they spent together during Jesus' earthly ministry, those apostles would have come to know each other well. They would have become good friends, laughing together and enjoying each other's company on their travels from town to town. They would have experienced a lot of togetherness while they walked, ate, and discussed the days' activities with Jesus and with each other. They would have known each other's strengths, as well as weaknesses and faults. In three years you can get to know a person quite well!

Not only did they get to know *each other* well, they also had the privilege of getting to know the Lord Jesus better than anyone else could have. Daily they could observe Jesus' mannerisms and habits as they lived with Him twenty-four hours a day. They heard Jesus preach and teach to crowds. They saw how He treated people with compassion. They heard His unforgettable parables and stories that captivated large audiences. They had observed the Master caring for hungry people by twice miraculously providing food for thousands of them. They had witnessed countless healings of sick people and had even watched Him raise the dead to life. They saw Jesus in moments of leisure, as well as under stress.

The disciples observed integrity and wisdom embodied in the Master such as they had never seen before. But no matter how well they thought they knew Jesus, they also discovered that He was unpredictable. He often caught them off guard. They must have marveled to see how Jesus cleverly answered His enemies and how He dared to confront the religious hierarchy. In fact, He seemed to fear no one.

The Lord Jesus shared power with His apostles. He empowered them to preach, as well as to heal and to cast out demons. These men were in the inner circle. Jesus shared the secrets of the Kingdom of God with them, secrets hidden in parables that were not always understood by the crowds. They would have witnessed more of Christ's miracles than anyone else simply because they were *with* Him more than anyone else. They would have attended services at the synagogue together and gone to the great Temple at Jerusalem. They saw how Jesus could attract huge crowds of people. But they also witnessed many people turning away from Jesus, disbelieving. The apostles and Jesus were a close-knit group.

Thus, it would be shocking to hear Jesus make a chilling prediction that *one* of these choice men who had been through so much with Him would soon betray Him. Such a thought would be unthinkable. "Truly, I say to you, one of you will betray me" (Matthew 26:21).

Matthew writes about their reaction to such news: ". . . they were very sorrowful, and began to say to Him one after the other, 'Is it I, Lord?'" (Matthew 26:22). Their response indicated a nervous, insecure uncertainty. Each one seemed unsure of his loyalty at this point. *No one* was bragging unshakeable devotion at this moment. This select group of apostles now had a dark cloud hanging over them.

How could any in this close group betray the Master, as He was predicting?

Jesus' revelation of what was to come took something away from the joy of this Passover meal for the apostles. Something was going wrong with the Jesus movement. Someone was trying to undermine the cause from within. The betrayer's hands were right there—on the table, according to the Master. "But behold the hand of him who betrays me is with me on the table" (Luke 22:21).

Only John's Gospel account picks up the *exit* of the betrayer. In response to Peter's questioning of the identity of the betrayer, Jesus responded.

> "It is he to whom I shall give this morsel when I have dipped it." So when He had dipped the morsel, He gave it to Judas, the son of Simon Iscariot. Then after the morsel, Satan entered into him. Jesus said to him, "What you are going to do, do quickly." So, after receiving the morsel, he immediately went out; and it was night. (John 13:26–30)

John adds in his Gospel that some of the apostles thought Judas was leaving the room to buy more food, since he was treasurer of the group. Jesus knew who His betrayer would be, even if the apostles could not guess. Judas was not yet a suspect. After all, Judas was the one entrusted with great responsibility; he handled the money. How could such a person betray that trust for thirty pieces of silver? What a sell-out from someone in the inner circle! What went wrong here?

In Judas Iscariot we see a man even Jesus failed to reach by word or deed. Such a tragic end for a disciple of Christ who had been among the privileged few! "Even my bosom friend in whom I trusted, who ate of my bread, has lifted his heel against me," the Messianic prophesy had foretold of this shocking occurrence (Psalm 41:9). Surely Jesus must have wondered what *more* He could have done to reach Judas so that he would have remained loyal and faithful. He had to feel a deep sense of hurt in such betrayal.

Jesus did not try to restrain Judas from leaving, even though He knew what Judas was going to do. How sad it must have been for Jesus to see a friend abandoning Him, knowing that their relationship would never be the same again.

Since the betrayer couldn't live with himself after betraying Jesus, he committed suicide. After Jesus' Ascension to heaven, the disciples felt that a replacement for Judas was necessary and another man was chosen. The remaining men drew lots to determine who it would be, ". . . and the lot fell on Matthias; and he was enrolled with the eleven apostles" (Acts of the Apostles 1:26).

How could Judas stoop so low yet be so foolish? Still, Jesus did not try to stop him or to humiliate him before the other apostles. Jesus told Judas privately, "What you are going to do, do quickly" (John 13:27).

Judas was not acting on his own. Judas had another master; that was the problem. The Scriptures explain that clearly when they say, "Then Satan entered into Judas Iscariot" (Luke 22:3). Jesus once said, "No one can serve two masters" (Matthew 6:24). Satan was the mastermind behind this evil betrayal by Judas. What happened is more than a traitorous deed of a weak apostle. What happened was Satanic. "Satan entered into Judas . . ." Judas was possessed.

Judas did repent of His betrayal, but it was too late for the consequences to be reversed. He never returned to Jesus. He tried to return the silver and undo his deed, but the religious leaders rejected it. Judas never sought mercy and forgiveness from the Master. In despair, he took his life by hanging. What a wasted life! Judas died without a friend. The mere mention of his name still sends chills to believers.

"It would have been better for that man if he had not been born" (Matthew 26:24). *What an epitaph!*

Still, for the one man whom Jesus was unable to reach in the inner circle, there were eleven others Jesus *did* reach, eleven faithful men who had shared in that first Communion and whose names are on the lips of Christians today: Peter, James, John, Andrew, Phillip, Thomas, Matthew, Bartholomew, James (the son of Alphaeus), Thaddeus, Simon the Zealot. Add to these Matthias, who took Judas' place, and there were still twelve. Jesus might have failed to reach Judas Iscariot but He has and is reaching billions of others. His death was not in vain!

If you are one of Jesus' followers and disciples, you are now a privileged person. *You* are invited into the inner circle. Jesus Christ invites you to His table to share in the bread and the cup of celebration and remembrance—just as did the apostles of long ago. Receive the bread and cup with gratitude. You and I may fail to reach some people. But there are many others Jesus is calling us to reach.

Many will respond to our efforts. It's not a lost cause by any means. It's an eternal cause with victory at the end. "For as often as you eat this bread and drink this cup, you proclaim the Lord's death until He comes" (1 Corinthians 11:26).

The apostles heard it first. We can still hear the sacred words today at His table, "This is my body which is given for you. Do this in remembrance of me . . . This cup, which is poured out for you, is the new covenant in my blood" (Luke 22:19–20).

Chapter Nine

THE UNREPENTANT THIEF

"One of the criminals who were hanged railed at Him, saying, 'Are you not the Christ? Save yourself and us!' But the other rebuked him . . ."

—Luke 23:39–40

King Jesus, riding triumphantly into Jerusalem on a lowly donkey amidst public cheering in the streets by crowds of jubilant people on the first Palm Sunday, is later contrasted to the King of the Jews, dying on a cross of disgrace along with two thieves at a Roman public execution.

Suddenly the focus in the Gospel accounts shifts from an image of Jesus lifted up as a success by the crowds on Palm Sunday to Jesus' inability to convert one individual thief dying on a cross beside Him. In fact, there were two—one on each side. One of the thieves became a believer; the other thief remained unconvinced to the end and cynically scorned the Crucified One who claimed to be the Messianic King.

One rejected; one embraced faith in Jesus. How different these two thieves were!

Jesus' few preserved words from the Cross only ampli-fied the sermon He was preaching in word and in deed by dying to save the world from sin.

The last lofty pulpit of the Great Evangelist Jesus be-fore His death was not from a fisherman's boat, not from grassy slopes overlooking the beautiful Sea of Galilee, not from a local synagogue, nor at the sacred Temple in Jerusa-lem. Jesus' last pulpit before His death was certainly not some distinguished marble pulpit in a majestic cathedral. Jesus' last pulpit for sermon and prayer was a crude, wooden cross in an awful, outdoor place called Golgotha, the place of the skull.

The event was a public execution of criminals by Roman soldiers outside the walls of the busy, ancient city of Jerusa-lem. "The Seven Last Words of Jesus," uttered in pain, sum-marized Jesus' last sermon and prayers for the world to hear; brief, profound words, which over the centuries have inspired countless Lenten sermons and Good Friday services.

But the sermon Jesus was preaching from the Cross was more than words. He Himself was the sermon, the Word— a profound sermon, written in Blood, proclaiming salva-tion through His suffering and death. Naturally, as with all sermons, not everyone got the message. Rarely do *all* hear-ers of a sermon understand it, no matter how good it is.

Jesus used to make the following observation about some hearers of His parables and teachings, quoting a prophet of old: "You shall indeed hear but never under-stand, and you shall indeed see but never perceive" (Mat-thew 13:14; See also Isaiah 6:9).

Not only would many fail to understand Jesus' words; many would also fail to understand His life, His death . . . He was the Word of God.

And the Word became flesh and dwelt among us, full of grace and truth; we have beheld His glory, glory as of the only Son from the Father. (John 1:14)

There were three crosses the day Jesus was executed at the hands of Roman soldiers by order of Pontius Pilate. In the eyes of many, all three crosses supported criminals, enemies of the people. If so many regarded Jesus as a criminal, what effect could His last sermon have? Who would be impressed by a sermon preached by a criminal on death row?

But not all regarded Jesus as a criminal deserving of death. Certainly His mother, His apostles, and His followers all knew otherwise. It was they who remembered His last words on the Cross and recorded them for posterity— just as though Jesus had dictated the words on tape. The apostles would remember the words He spoke at the First Communion in the Upper Room. Neither would they ever forget the words Jesus preached and lived.

One of the thieves crucified with Jesus *did* become a believer and asked Jesus to remember him when He entered His Kingdom. Particularly at a moment like this, *that was faith.* Jesus answered the new convert's request with these famous, reassuring words from the Cross, "Truly, I say to you, today you will be with me in Paradise" (Luke 23:43).

But such success in evangelism from this last pulpit was overshadowed by Jesus' inability to reach the other thief, who defiantly refused to be so easily won over. No deathbed repentance for him. Instead, the Scripture account says that he "railed" against Jesus: "One of the criminals who were hanged railed at Him, saying, 'Are you not the Christ? Save yourself and us'" (Luke 23:39).

This thief only mocked and scorned the Great Evangelist, denouncing Jesus as powerless unless He could rescue them from dying. Only immediate deliverance would convince him. The unbelieving thief saw the same thing the converted thief saw. Both men saw the Word on the Cross. Both could hear Jesus. The unbelieving thief saw, but didn't see; he heard, but didn't hear.

The same words, the same life, seen by two thieves . . . but only one believed. The fault for the rejection is not in the one who speaks the Word but in the one who wills not to believe. Jesus did not only preach truth. He *was* Truth. In Jesus' own words, "I am the way, and the truth, and the life . . ." (John 14:6).

The unrepentant thief could not see how Jesus as King could ever liberate the world from bondage if He could not liberate the three of them from the fate of Crucifixion. The late Bishop Fulton Sheen once said that one thief asked to be taken up while the other asked to be taken down. Why is it that one man could see Christ's eternal Kingdom while the other man could see only supposedly false, grandiose claims?

"He has blinded their eyes and hardened their heart, lest they should see with their eyes and perceive with their hearts, and turn for me to heal them" (John 12:40). Many today still suffer from "spiritual blindness," bitterly rejecting Jesus as their Savior even to the end.

I have heard some Christians protest and resent God's acceptance of "deathbed repentance." Can even Christians resent God's loving and forgiving nature? Do such resentful Christians prefer persistent, unrepentant defiance of God's salvation to the end? Jesus once told people that repentance brings *joy* to heaven, saying, ". . . there will be more joy in heaven over one sinner who repents than over ninety-nine righteous persons who need no repentance" (Luke 15:7).

The hymn writer Earl Marlatt reminds us of this in his beloved hymn, "Are Ye Able?" written in 1926. The song lyric asks, poignantly, "Are ye able to remember, when a thief lifts up his eyes, that his pardoned soul is worthy of a place in paradise?"

How can two people go to the same church, attend the same evangelistic crusade, hear the same sermon, and react totally differently? One person goes away responding in faith; the other only scoffs the preacher and the sermon. How can two people watch the same religious program on TV and react differently—one positively, the other negatively?

How can two persons both be raised in the same home with the same believing parents, yet one becomes a committed Christian and worker in the church while the other repudiates organized religion and faith, preferring willful defiance and unbelief? Maybe the blame is not with the church or with fine Christian parents. The blame is certainly not with Jesus Christ, who was "without sin" (Hebrews 4:15).

Any failure to reach people and touch their lives was Jesus' own self-limitation. He would never *force* anyone to believe in Him nor to repent. If Jesus fails to reach a person, it is due to a failure of *the person* to respond to the Word, to understand truth, to believe, or to change. Many fail to respond to the offer of God's amazing grace. Even in prison, some change for good and repent. Others never change.

In any kind of rehabilitation program, one can have success with one person and failure with another, even where both receive the same treatment. Results depend on the individual person. Many people had the chance to see King Jesus in action those three years of His ministry. They saw Him healing, preaching and teaching, confronting sin and hypocrisy. Many had the chance to see Jesus' beautiful life, glowing in holiness and kindness, yet not all of those who saw Him believed.

The two thieves on crosses beside Jesus could see the Savior close-up. Previous to that day, those two thieves probably never saw Jesus in action. They had missed so much and knew so little about Jesus. But on the day of the Crucifixion one of the two thieves recognized greatness. One saw Truth with his own eyes. One saw hope and a new Kingdom coming with Christ as its King.

One saw innocence. The other thief could see only a fraud; another person living a false life such as he himself had led. If he could not see a miracle, could not be freed from his cross, he could see no Kingdom. The unrepentant thief ignored even the rebuke by the believing thief. The believing thief failed to convince the unbeliever. Why success with one thief and failure with another? Conditions were the same for both.

This question is always perplexing. The only conclusion we can make is that people respond differently to similar events. Jesus won one thief for His Kingdom and lost the other, who didn't want to be won. Jesus was only 50 per cent successful with the two men. Jesus never said everyone would respond positively to His invitations. In fact, He seemed to say that results of evangelism would be hard fought: "For the gate is narrow and the way is hard, that leads to life, and those who find it are few" (Matthew 7:14).

The unrepentant thief saw the drama as a tragic comedy— a picture of shattered, imagined greatness and power in a dying man who claimed to be a King. He scornfully sneered at this pathetic picture of three helpless, dying men on crosses without hope. The tortured, unrepentant thief was not about to mellow. No one would ever be able to say that *he* made a deathbed repentance. He held out in bold defiance to the bitter end. His life ended, scorning the Messianic King.

The unrepentant thief demanded immediate liberation, not only as proof of King Jesus' credentials, but also because he felt worthy of freedom, entitled to the right of liberation. He set a deadline for the rescue that didn't leave much time. His life as a thief demonstrated that he felt he had a right to take for himself what belonged to others. The believing thief, on the other hand, knew that he was guilty and that he was only getting what he deserved. He knew that Jesus was the only innocent one among them. He rebuked the unrepentant thief.

> Do you not fear God, since you are under the same sentence of condemnation? And we justly; for we are receiving the due reward of our deeds; but this man (Jesus) has done nothing wrong. (Luke 23:40–41)

How close can one get to Jesus and still not turn to Him? What must it have been like to die next to Jesus? The two thieves could not have gotten any closer to Him than this. Jesus did not die alone; they were fellow sufferers with Him. You would think this closeness to death's door would be enough to make one think deeply and make some effort to get right with God.

The story seems to illustrate that it is *never too late* to turn to Jesus and repent of one's past. This is the beauty of grace and forgiveness. But the story also illustrates how foolish people can be, refusing to change to their last breath. The Christian church does fail to reach some people, no matter how many prayers are lifted up for the salvation of others, no matter how loving and persuasive one can be, no matter how fine an example is set.

Right up to the end, some go out of this world into eternity cursing faith and goodness, scorning love and humility as weakness, rejecting truth as falsehood, refusing eternal life and mocking Divine Judgment as fiction. How moving it is to watch both King Jesus and the believing thief, unable together to evangelize the unrepentant thief. Some people, even in old age, refuse to mellow in pride, even when death is close at hand.

My wife and I recently visited Squam Lake in Northern New Hampshire, where the 1981 motion picture *On Golden Pond*, starring the late Henry Fonda and Katherine Hepburn was filmed. The movie showed how crotchety, old Norman Thayer could be and how only his wife, Ethel, could see through all his gruffness and ill-natured crudeness to the good lying dormant just beneath the surface of the man.

In the film, the old man at his New England cottage on the lake was determined to be mean and tough with his daughter, Chelsea, and her boyfriend (and even her son), but mellows by the end of the film. He changes, and it makes us feel good to see redemptive change in a stubborn, difficult personality.

The believing thief didn't know much about Jesus, the King. He was only going by the *little* he knew. With what little he knew about the King, he realized without a doubt that he wanted to be included in Jesus' Kingdom. The believing thief didn't even get baptized. He didn't know much theology and Bible. But he knew the King would get them through all this to the other side in paradise. The unrepentant thief had the same chance but lost it because of unbelief.

Maybe the lesson in all of this is that we should not let the unrepentant discourage us from reaching out to others who *will* respond to the Gospel. Jesus Himself talked about a huge harvest just waiting to be brought in. "The harvest is plentiful," He said, but the laborers are few; pray therefore the Lord of the harvest to send out laborers into His harvest" (Matthew 9:37–38).

Someone is out there waiting for you and me. Someone is just waiting for an invitation, a word of welcome, a word of encouragement and support, a word about King Jesus and His Kingdom. Go out into the world expectantly, as ministers of the Gospel. Go in peace and bear fruit, remembering our Lord's words: "You did not choose me, but I chose you, and appointed you that you should go and bear fruit and that your fruit should abide" (John 15:16).

Chapter Ten

THE MILITARY

> *"And the soldiers led Him away inside the palace (that is, the praetorium) and they called together the whole battalion. And they clothed Him in a purple cloak, and plaiting a crown of thorns they put it on Him. And they began to salute Him, 'Hail, King of the Jews!' And they struck His head with a reed, and spat upon Him, and they knelt down in homage to Him. And when they had mocked Him, they stripped Him of the purple cloak, and put His own clothes on Him. And they led Him out to crucify Him."*
>
> —Mark 15:16–20

Soldiers do what they have to do. They are under orders. The Roman soldiers had a job to do—to crucify three men, one of whom was Jesus Christ.

Before they carried out their gruesome task of execution, the soldiers had some fun at Jesus' expense. They made a mockery of Jesus' claim to be a king. They mocked and joked while guarding Him before the public execution. They spit on Him, then knelt down like they were honoring a King. As part of the mockery, they made Jesus wear a crown of thorns and a purple robe. They even saluted Him and shouted praise to Him, saying, "Hail, King of the Jews!" They hit Jesus on the head with grassy reeds to humiliate Him further.

Their mockery lacked any semblance of reverence or respect. What they were doing, they were doing ignorantly. No wonder Jesus prayed for God's mercy upon the clueless tormenters while He hung on the Cross, "Father, forgive them; for they know not what they do" (Luke 23:34).

There were no mass conversions of soldiers the day of the Crucifixion. They just did their duty, what they were told to do.

How could the soldiers be so callous? They had no choice. These soldiers were not necessarily evil men. They were sons of *someone*. Many would have been sweethearts or husbands. Some would have been fathers. They were patriotic and were doing their duty to their country. They were keeping law and order. They had no idea who Jesus really was or the good He had done.

In their eyes, the three to be executed deserved what they were going to get. They must have believed that Jesus and the other two were lawless men disturbing the peace. Society must be rid of such men and soldiers must do the unpleasant task. Orders had been given to execute all three.

How could Jesus hope to reach the soldiers or to convince them He was right and society was wrong? After all, the execution not only had the authority of the State behind it. Jesus' execution also had the blessing of organized religion, the sanction of the High Priest. Crowds within the community had demanded Jesus' death as a criminal. *Does society sometimes go mad because of ignorance?*

Jesus was unable to win over all the soldiers who guarded Him but the Gospel accounts tell about one soldier, an officer, a Centurion, who could sort things out for himself and could see that Jesus was an innocent man. Luke's Gospel tells that (Luke 23:47).

Mark's Gospel also tells us that the Centurion said, "Truly this man was the Son of God!" That is a statement of faith. Matthew's Gospel says that others guarding Jesus also could see who Jesus was and said, "Truly this was the Son of God!" (See Mark 15:39, Matthew 27:54). Not all the soldiers were blind to truth.

Earlier in Jesus' ministry another Roman Centurion at Capernaum had so much faith in Him that he believed Jesus would only have to speak the word and his beloved servant, who was dying, would be restored. Jesus was so overwhelmed with that kind of faith in a Gentile military man that He had to admit He hadn't seen faith like that in His own people of Israel (Luke 7:1–10).

The soldiers guarding Jesus would have been extremely hard to convince. They were used to the grim business of crucifixion, of driving nails through bleeding hands and feet followed by hours of standing guard while their victims died in slow, tortured agony. Mocking Jesus before the Cross provided some laughter amidst their gruesome task. How could Jesus get through to laughing soldiers?

As difficult as it was to reach the soldiers, so too, it may be just as difficult today to reach modern people. There are similarities in the lack of openness to Jesus Christ and the spiritual truth He offers.

First of all, the soldiers did what they did because they were told to do it. They were not to question official orders. They were under pressure. Many in Hitler's Nazi Germany said the same thing. They said they were only following orders. Maybe many in our society do the same. They don't question culture or patriotism. They just blindly follow leaders and the crowd.

Social pressure keeps people stuck in conformity. "Everybody's doing it." Many young people today stay away from church because their friends and peers aren't going and because many parents just don't go to church anymore. If their families, friends, and neighbors don't go to church, social pressure wins as people "join the crowd." Who wants to be different?

Who wants to be the only ones on the block to go to church? Many parents keep their children home from Sunday school and church even though Jesus Christ told the disciples not to keep the children away from Him, saying, "Let the children come to me, and do not hinder them" (Luke 18:16).

Sunday Schools and churches would be full today if moms and dads brought their children instead of indifferently staying home.

The soldiers made fun of religion when they mocked Jesus as King. It may be as hard to reach fun-loving Americans as it would have been for Jesus to have reached those Roman soldiers. Church today gets low priority when competing with sports, parties, fun weekends, shows, the malls, TV, yard, garden, and house improvement, family gatherings, and vacation time. How can a Sunday School Bible Study or church service compete with secular culture? How can a volunteer choir in a small church compete with modern music professionalism on TV or on stage?

Soldiers gambled for Jesus' seamless garment. Rather than tearing His garment into pieces, they would keep it in one piece and gamble for it, a souvenir of the day to take home. The soldiers were so preoccupied with gambling for Jesus' outer seamless garment that they missed what Jesus was all about. They missed salvation because their focus was wrong. Materialism overshadowed spirituality. John's Gospel reminds us of their obsession with winning what Jesus was wearing.

But the tunic was without seam, woven from top to bottom; so that they said to one another, "Let us not tear it, but cast lots for it to see whose it shall be." So the soldiers did this. (John 19:23–25)

The winner took Jesus' garment home with him. What did he then do with his winnings? Did he wear it the next day or did he hang it up to show others his prize trophy? How sad to be the winner of the garment Jesus had worn and to miss what the Savior had to offer—salvation itself. The "lucky" winner lost what he might have gained.

Americans love to gamble! The lotteries, the races, the casinos, the sweepstakes, or the stock market become an obsession and a preoccupation for many. Many Americans get more pleasure and excitement out of gambling than out of going to church. Many complain that church bores them, that it is dull. Have you ever watched people pull the levers endlessly on casino machines? Have you noticed that today's winners are often tomorrow's losers? Every day, people gamble away far more than they would ever think of giving to church or to charity. What if the money could have been placed on Sunday's offering plate, a gamble on God's Kingdom? Jesus said it so well long ago when He taught us, "For where your treasure is, there will be your heart also" (Matthew 6:21).

The soldiers had another job to do after the Crucifixion. They were ordered to stand guard over Jesus' sealed tomb to make sure no one took His dead body away and then make the claim that He had come back to life.

Conservative *traditionalists* can be as hard to reach as the soldiers. The soldiers stood guard over the tomb, trying to protect the status quo. They were guarding the dead King. A *sealed* tomb was meant to guarantee that no one would remove Jesus' body. The soldiers were there to make sure nothing changed.

Some conservative people are so afraid of change that they would rather preserve their copy of a dusty, unused *Family Bible* than to open their hearts and minds to new truth. It is as hard to reach a person who is resisting change in his or her lifestyle as it would have been to reach soldiers whose job it was to make sure there was no talk of Resurrection by guarding Jesus' tomb after His burial. It is just as hard to change the mind of a person who says, "We never did it that way before."

The soldiers did their best to keep the tomb sealed. But an earthquake shook the earth and an angel from God moved the stone away from the tomb. The soldiers could not stop the Resurrection of King Jesus. They could only watch something happen before their stunned eyes. They could only rush back to the authorities and tell them something had happened out there at the tomb, something beyond the imagination! If the Risen Christ could not reach the soldiers, how can we expect to reach many who are trying to guard tombs of spiritual death and who resist revival and new life in Christ? It may be as difficult to reach apathetic church members who have been "on the church rolls" for years and are known as "dead wood" as it is to reach prodigal unbelievers.

The soldiers were willing to do anything for money. They often accepted bribe money—hush money. They would often accept shekels under the table. Yes, it was well known that extra money above a soldier's salary would cause him to compromise truth.

These men could be bought not to tell what really happened at the tomb. According to Matthew's Gospel, religious leaders offered the soldiers money with the condition that they tell people that Jesus' disciples came while the soldiers were sleeping and stole the body.

"So they took the money and did as they were directed" (Matthew 28:15)

Many in our society today are also willing to do anything for a price. Some push drugs—for money. Some steal—for money. Some young people enter prostitution—for money. Some get involved with pornography—for money. Some cheat, lie, or even kill—for money. Some are bought in business and political corruption. Greed makes affluent people indifferent to needs of others and the poor. Nations go to war—often for money. As they say, if you want to understand what motivates someone, "follow the money trail." Many would sell their very souls—for money.

Many would see a church's appeal for money as a threat. I believe many stay away from church and religion because they fear being asked to part with some of their money. The love of money often holds back the advancement of the Kingdom of God. It's hard to reach people who compromise truth and integrity for money.

"For the love of money is the root of all evils" (1 Timothy 6:10).

Christ sends us Christians out into our communities to win people for Him. As we go, many *will* respond to our efforts. Someone is waiting for you and for me. Someone needs you to come! Christ is risen. Tell someone. Tell the world about the Good News of salvation through faith in Christ. Tell your family. Tell your friends. Tell your neighbors and your acquaintances. Tell the stranger. Tell the enemy.

Don't stop with a Christmas Eve service. Don't stop with an Easter celebration. Keep the joy alive! Help to fill Christ's church on Sunday morning. Bring someone to church. Give a Bible to someone. Get excited. Christ is risen! Let us rise with Him.

Christ promised that His followers would be able to do even *greater things* than He was doing. That is an incredible concept, yet His words were clear when He said, "Truly, truly, I say to you, he who believes in me will also do the works that I do; and greater works than these will he do, because I go to the Father" (John 14:12).

So don't get discouraged when you can't reach *some* people. Even Jesus wasn't able to reach everyone. Why should He expect you to be able to reach everyone if He couldn't? He doesn't. But He does expect us to keep trying. The Lord sends us to others who can be reached. Keep hope alive!

King Jesus was unable to reach many people only because He refused to coerce people to believe in Him. Jesus sought Love and Faith as a response and He knew you can't force either. Jesus did not believe in forced religion. Therefore, the Messianic King voluntarily made Himself *vulnerable to rejection* by the nonviolent self-limitation of His power and authority.

Jesus Christ, though He was King, restrained His own power to ensure that people were free to choose whether to follow Him or not. People had the freedom to reject the Savior or to love Him and follow Him. His followers must remember that some people will choose not to follow Christ. But His followers must also remember that many people are ready to choose to follow Christ if someone will just share the Good News with them.

> So faith comes from what is heard, and what is heard comes by the preaching of Christ. (Romans 10:17)

Let us hold fast our faith that God loves this world and that His Son, out of love, died for sinners. Anyone who can understand and appreciate such love will love God and will also love His Son, Jesus.

Epilogue

If Jesus Christ Himself was unable to persuade every one He tried to reach with the Gospel, why should we Christian church people, with all our imperfections, be surprised today when we also fail to get through to those who reject our efforts? Neither should we contemporary Christians be surprised when our efforts are well-received and welcomed because, like the Master, success comes to us at the time appointed.

For all those who walk away, there are others who are eager to follow Christ and who accept our invitation to become committed Christians. In spite of discouragements along life's spiritual pilgrimage there are also many rewarding experiences of seeing people respond to our some-times—clumsy efforts at evangelism. Just to hear one child singing "Jesus Loves Me" because of our efforts is worth it all, isn't it?

What if someone rejects our efforts? Someone else, an-other voice crying in the wilderness, may still be able to reach them. That is a thought, and it ought to be in our prayers. *Lord, if I am unable to reach this one for you, please allow someone else to do so in the future.*

All you and I can do is to try to do our best for God—and leave people in His hands. The *effort* is what is important to God. Jesus Christ made that effort. We should follow in His steps. Thank God for Christians who make the effort to touch the lives of others for Christ.

A good prayer for us imperfect Christians to pray in our attempts to evangelize the world around us is a prayer I once heard when I was in seminary at the Theological School at Drew University in the late fifties. The late Frank C. Laubach, famed world literacy missionary, spoke. I never forgot his simple prayer before his message to us students. "Bless all that is Thine. Forgive all that is mine."

Though we may fail to reach all the people we would like to reach, we can expect to touch many others who will respond positively to the Gospel, even as Jesus reached the Repentant Thief. There are always people who will believe and change. Isn't that exciting? Isn't it worth it to try to reach people, knowing that some *will* respond positively? Some will gladly become disciples of Christ and will be active in His Church. Isn't it wonderful to be part of the process of shepherding that wins people to the King?

Isn't it good that someone didn't give up on you but helped to welcome you into Christ's Kingdom? I thank the Lord for all who encouraged and inspired me along the way in the Christian walk and helped me to see King Jesus. I thank all who not only introduced me to the Savior/King but also helped me understand more and more of the Bible truths that tell about Him and about our wonderful Heavenly Father who sent His Son to save us!

Thank God for Christ's Church, however imperfect it may be. Thank God that we have churches where we can go to worship and meet our brothers and sisters in Christ. Thank God for faithful pastors, Sunday school teachers, evangelists, missionaries, and supportive churchgoers who let their lights shine. Thank God for our Bibles, for excellent religious books and magazines, for religious music on tape, radio, and religious TV. All this is available to us because some believers have wanted to share their faith with their world. Therefore, go forth in boldness, proclaiming God's truth. That's how Jesus handled rejection!

Chapter Summaries and Study Guide

See How Jesus Handled Rejection!

By Gerald H. Ihle

Chapter One: The Rejected Cornerstone

Jesus had made grim predictions that He would have to experience rejection. Here Jesus was talking openly about failure. But when He was talking about Himself as the Cornerstone, which eventually becomes the chief stone in the building, He was not talking failure. He was talking ultimate success and victory. Jesus was fully aware of reality and what it would hold for His own future when He predicted that the Cornerstone would be rejected.

Even so, the Cornerstone, Jesus Christ, has been welcomed by countless millions of believers over the years.

Identify where the Cornerstone is rejected in today's world. What are the consequences of that rejection? Why did most of the opposition to Jesus come from religious leaders?

99

See How Jesus Handled Rejection!

Why would Jesus prepare His followers for resistance and rejection when perhaps more would have followed Him if He had promised them success and victory?

Chapter Two: His Own People

Jesus knew the frustration of being rejected at home among His own people. Jesus failed to win His own community and religious home base, the Holy City, Jerusalem, the home of the great Temple. Jesus did not stop trying to reach His people just because He was often met with rejection. Many of the Jews *did* become convinced believers and followed Him faithfully. The modern Church needs to be reminded of the rewards of persistence. For every failure to reach someone, some other person may be eager to respond in faith.

How can Christians get over emphasizing the negative and begin emphasizing the positive hope of reaching the reachable?

Why wasn't Jesus accepted by His own people?

Why is it so hard to overcome spiritual blindness and ignorance?

Why is the way to peace so hidden and elusive?

Why did Jesus send the disciples to the Jews first before He sent them to the Gentiles?

If Jesus couldn't convince His own people, how could He be expected to convince an unbelieving Gentile world?

How do Christians sometimes treat Jesus with disrespectful familiarity?

If Jesus, with His many strengths, couldn't win everyone He met to His side, should Christians, with weaknesses and imperfections, expect to do more?

What does this author say overcomes the inertia that comes with discouragement over rejection?

Chapter Three: The Samaritans

This chapter reminds us that Jesus was able to reach some Samaritans, but one Samaritan village in particular refused to welcome Him. Because of its rude refusal, James and John wanted to destroy it with fire, an example of *conditional* love. Jesus exemplified *unconditional* love and would have none of the disciples' eagerness for destruction. He directed them to move on to another more hospitable place.

The Samaritan town closed the door on Jesus, but their defiance did not mean that Jesus would then allow an unchristian crusade of death and destruction to be showered on them by zealous disciples who could not understand Jesus' unconditional love for the townspeople.

Many today also misunderstand the loving Christ because of unloving Christians, who tragically misrepresent the real Jesus. Christians need to keep the love flowing unconditionally, as our Lord Jesus did.

In what areas of your contacts can you show more unconditional love toward others?

Differentiate between conditional *and* unconditional *love. Give an example of each.*

What labels on people today should Christians disregard (as Jesus disregarded labels) as they reach out to all kinds of people?

How did Jesus answer James and John when they wanted Jesus' blessing to "firebomb" unbelievers, like the prophet Elijah had done in the Old Testament?

When Jesus' followers are rejected and unwelcome, what are we to do?

Chapter Four: The Rich Man

The story of the rich man walking away from Jesus reveals to us one reason some people turn away from a church's efforts to evangelize them. Sometimes the cost seems just too great. Jesus saw how riches stood in the way for this particular man. It was not Jesus who initiated the dialogue between Himself and the rich man; this man asked Christ what he lacked.

The rich man walked away and we don't even know his name. His name could have been added to the names of great men in the Bible who had been a part of salvation history-in-the-making!

People seem to fear Jesus' call to discipleship because of what they might have to give up—and it's not just money. It might be grudges, pride, racism, comforts, time, self-pity, an addiction, a moral deviation or indifference to human suffering. The story ends sadly.

The rich man was not an enemy. Jesus' call here was rejected by a good man, a moral man. The rich man had one lack. Don't we all? That doesn't stop Jesus from reaching out to touch us and to invite us into His Kingdom. Love and grace are offered freely, not forcibly. Jesus doesn't force His way into a person's life uninvited.

Is it possible that there are people today who are so focused on acquiring wealth that they see Christ and His Church as an intrusion and a threat to their greed?

Why do you suppose Jesus would not compromise and settle for a tithe promise from the rich man who would have made a good disciple?

What did Jesus offer the rich man in exchange for giving away his wealth?

Besides wealth, what else do people fear giving up in order to be a follower of Christ?

What interests possess wealthy people most and what do they enjoy talking about endlessly?

Why doesn't Jesus force Himself more on people and why does He honor free, personal choice and the opportunity to reject what He offers?

Is recruitment for ministry today more difficult because gifted young people seek more promising financial rewards, greater advancements, and prestige in the secular world?

Chapter Five: Hypocrites—Blind Guides

Jesus was confrontational with religious leaders of His day, daring to call them "self-righteous hypocrites and blind guides." The religious leaders accused Jesus of blasphemy, but not of hypocrisy. Religious leaders made Jesus angry because He knew they should be setting the example for the faithful and for secular culture. He rebuked them openly for their hypocritical judgments of others. This did not make Jesus popular with the religious elite!

Jesus was harder on religious hypocrites than He was on immoral sinners, thieves, tax collectors, political leaders, or rich oppressors. Jesus saw pride and self-righteousness, the false appearance of virtue, as sin. Jesus removed the masks of moral superiority from the angry Pharisees. Even today, self-righteous people are the hardest to change because they are blind to their own faults and are harsh, unforgiving judges of others. Jesus knew spiritual blindness makes people hateful.

What was Jesus never accused here of being?

Why was Jesus more confrontational with religious leaders about being hypocritical than He was with political leaders or with the oppressive rich?

What keeps hypocrites from seeing their own faults, and why are self-righteous people such harsh critics and judges of others?

How did Jesus deal with the men who felt morally justified in stoning a woman caught in an adulterous affair?

What would it take to break down and humble a proud, self-righteous hypocrite?

If we all have blind spots, how can we identify what the blind spots are and can those blind spots be corrected?

Chapter Six: Leaders of Religion and Government

It took the united efforts of organized religion and State, of Jew and Gentile, to authorize the Crucifixion. Any Gentile who wants to blame the Crucifixion totally on the Jews is ignorantly wrong, conveniently forgetting that the actual torture and death of Jesus on the Cross was done by Gentile soldiers and ordered by a Gentile Governor, Pontius Pilate. Neither Temple nor State would grant sanctuary for "the King of the Jews." No one stood up for Jesus. No one pleaded on His behalf. World leaders of religions and governments today still exert great influence and control over the people they lead and govern. That powerful and authoritative influence can be a formidable obstacle to evangelism. Religious and Government leaders can still be the hardest to reach because of their prestigious and powerful positions.

Would world leaders of religion and government today welcome Jesus any more than those years ago who together approved the Crucifixion of Jesus?

Why have world religions feared religious freedom, religious tolerance, and free debate and questioning in the search for truth?

What makes religious people feel sometimes that they are doing God a favor by killing people in His name?

What can turn proud, self-righteous, successful, rich leaders of government and religion into humble disciples of Christ, ready to learn and obey?

Chapter Seven: Satan, "the Devil"

God's strategy that would end Satan's rule on earth sounded like a strategy doomed to failure. Jesus talked about how He would have to suffer and die in order to fulfill His mission. The battle plan sounded awful!

When Jesus talked about this plan, Peter once scolded Him for saying such a thing. The disciples wanted nothing less than success from their Messiah. All during Jesus' three-year ministry of word and deed He failed to persuade Satan, who remained unrepentant and unrelenting. Satan didn't want to be saved and would remain Jesus' greatest enemy. Jesus couldn't convert this enemy of heaven and earth, the great adversary of God and God's people.

Satan was one enemy even Jesus could not love. Satan hated God and was trying to destroy everyone Jesus loved and wanted to save.

Why didn't God destroy Satan long ago? Why does God allow Satan to continue to exist and to lead people astray and cause such destruction and death?

Why was Satan one enemy Jesus could not love?

What plan of Satan backfired?

Will Satan eventually be killed or condemned to torment? (See The Book of Revelation.)

According to Martin Luther's hymn, "A Mighty Fortress is Our God" what is the "one little word" that will cause Satan's downfall?

Chapter Eight: Judas Iscariot

In Judas Iscariot, we see a trusted disciple who turned against Jesus. This was such a tragic end for a disciple of Christ who had been among the privileged few. How sad it must have been for Jesus to see a friend abandon Him, knowing it would never be the same again! But for the one Jesus was unable to reach in the inner circle, there were eleven faithful disciples Jesus *did* reach, in addition to Matthias, who took Judas' place.

Jesus may have failed to reach Judas Iscariot, but He would reach billions of others. His death was not in vain. You are now a privileged person if you are one of His followers and disciples. Jesus Christ invites you, as the disciples of long ago, into His inner circle and to His table to share in the bread and the cup of celebration and remembrance. You and I may fail to reach some people. But there are others Jesus is calling us to reach. Many will respond to our efforts!

Maybe Jesus is calling you or your church to reach out to someone. Who might that be?

What took away the joy of the Last Supper Passover meal?

Was Judas a suspect of betrayal when he left the table?

What does this Scripture mean? "Then Satan entered into Judas Iscariot" (Luke 22:3).

Chapter Nine: The Unrepentant Thief

In the Gospel account, the focus shifts from Jesus' successes with crowds, such as on Palm Sunday, to Jesus' inability to convert one individual thief dying on a cross. The sermon Jesus was preaching from the Cross was more than words. His life and death were the sermon. He Himself was the Word, a profound sermon, written in Blood, proclaiming salvation with His suffering and death.

Naturally, as with all sermons, not everyone got the message. Yet one of the thieves crucified with Jesus *did* become a believer and asked Jesus to remember Him when He entered His Kingdom. Still, such success in evangelism from this last pulpit was overshadowed by Jesus' inability to reach the *other* thief, who defiantly refused to be so easily won over.

The unrepentant thief saw the same thing that the converted thief had seen. How can two people go to the same church, the same evangelistic crusade, hear the same sermon, and react totally differently? Any failure to reach people and touch their lives was Jesus' own limit on Himself. He would never *force* anyone to believe or to repent. Jesus was only fifty percent successful with the two men.

How close can one get to Jesus and still reject Him?

What does the author mean when he says that Jesus Himself was "the Sermon, the Word" while He was on the Cross?

One thief knew very little about Jesus, yet he believed in Him. How much do you have to know about Jesus and the Bible to become a believer?

Chapter Ten: The Military

As difficult as it was to reach the soldiers, so too, it may be as difficult to reach people in the modern world today.

There are similarities in the lack of openness to Jesus Christ and spiritual truth in both ancient and modern eras. This chapter describes those similarities.

Identify similarities between modern society and the soldiers who crucified Jesus in their lack of openness and blindness to Jesus Christ and spiritual truth.

Does society sometimes go mad because of ignorance?

The Church today competes with modern culture. But how can a volunteer choir in a small church compete with modern, professional, highly paid musicians on TV or on stage?

If people like to gamble so much, why don't they gamble big time on Christ's Kingdom?

Why is it as difficult to reach apathetic "dead wood" church members as it is to reach prodigal unbelievers?

Why did Jesus make Himself vulnerable to rejection by His non-violent, self-imposed limitation on His own unlimited power?

How has this book influenced or inspired you? What new insights did it give to you?

If you have been part of a discussion group, how did your group help you to grow as a Christian?

To order additional copies of

See How Jesus Handled Rejection!

People Even Jesus Failed to Reach
With Interactive Study Guide

Have your credit card ready and call

Toll free: (877) 421-READ (7323)

or send $9.95* each plus $5.95 S&H** to

WinePress Publishing
PO Box 428
Enumclaw, WA 98022

or order online at: www.winepresspub.com

*WA residents, add 8.4% sales tax

**add $1.50 S&H for each additional book ordered